HOW I MADE A MILLION DOLLARS WITH A TOILET AND A CELL PHONE

How I Made a Million Dollars with a Toilet and a Cell Phone

How to Build a Business Online (Even When Life Hands You Crap)

Published by Game Changer Publishing

Paperback ISBN: 978-1-966659-31-0

Hardcover ISBN: 978-1-966659-32-7

Digital ISBN: 978-1-966659-33-4

GC GAME CHANGER PUBLISHING
www.GameChangerPublishing.com

DEDICATION

This book is for my family.

First, to my two siblings, True and Mikey: Thanks for riding the crazy entrepreneurship train with me since Day 1. Seriously, who else would stand for hours selling CDs and tortilla chips to random strangers at the state fair? Or help me sell candy in middle school until we get cut off by the principal? Or shoot random ridiculous videos while embarrassing ourselves in public just for fun? Nobody. You two are either super loyal or just have really bad judgment. Either way, I love you both.

To my mom: Thanks for showing me how to be a boss mom while working, chasing your dreams, and somehow keeping everything together. Thank you for stepping in during the toughest years to help me raise my son and allowing me the space to build my business. You never complained, and you never made me feel like a burden. I'll forever be grateful, but also slightly annoyed that you make multitasking look so easy. Thank you.
To my dad: for showing me hard work and for all the fun business ideas over the years. More importantly, thank you for being a great grandpa to London.

Thank you, Russell Brunson, who taught me how to take all of the chaos that was going on in my head and turn it into successful businesses that provide for me and my family. (I owe you a kidney)

And finally, to my incredible son. I love you more than words could ever express. You came into my life and lit a fire within me. Because of you, I had to rise up and get my act together. You pushed me to be more responsible, more determined, and more present, all so I could give you the best life possible. In doing so, you've given me an even greater life in return.

I'm endlessly proud of you and grateful every day that you chose me to be your mama.

You are my everything. Always.

And finally, this book is for anyone who is striving to create financial security for themselves and their loved ones while leaving a positive impact on the world.
Even when life feels impossibly hard, you have the choice to look at the things going on in your life as an unfortunate event, or an epic opportunity.

And if you're really struggling, just remember: you can cry while explaining it to your therapist or laugh about it on camera with your customers. One of these options costs you money, and the other one makes you money. There's no shame in therapy. But don't forget, laughing with your customers can be therapeutic, too... and it pays better.

And I'll tell ya, tears dry faster when you're holding a paycheck.

THANK YOU FOR READING MY BOOK!
DOWNLOAD YOUR FREE GIFTS

Just to say thanks for buying and reading my book, I'd like to give you a free bonus training below. This is how I created silly videos that brought in millions of views and millions in sales. I even cover a handful of ways you can make easy, funny ads for your business too, even if your business is boring, even if you're not creative or funny at all, and even if you have no idea where to start!
For the Free Training, Scan Below:

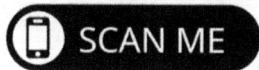

I appreciate your interest in my book and value your feedback as it helps me improve future versions of this book. I would appreciate it if you could leave your invaluable review on Amazon.com. Thank you!

HOW I MADE A MILLION DOLLARS WITH A TOILET AND A CELL PHONE

HOW TO BUILD A BUSINESS ONLINE
(EVEN WHEN LIFE HANDS YOU CRAP)

KRISTINE MIRELLE

CONTENTS

HOW THIS BOOK WORKS

Here's the deal: The first part of this book is all about *my* life and how I learned the lessons that led me to build my 7 figure businesses even as a busy mom. It's the messy, weird, sometimes ridiculous journey of how I figured out that funny ads could actually build a business (and make a life-changing amount of money).

BUT...

If you don't give a flying crap about that and are saying, "Just get to the part where you talk about how to make funny ads and how to sell stuff online," feel free to skip ahead to the 9 types of Funny Ads Chapter later in this book.

Either way, you're here. So buckle up. It's about to get weird.

INTRO:

MY LIFE WITH DRUG DEALERS AND PIMPS

Once upon a time, in Albuquerque, New Mexico, I found myself hanging out in a strip club with an interesting crew: two drug dealers (one was my boyfriend), a guy fresh out of prison after serving a life sentence for murder, and our friend, the local pimp. Not exactly where most "success stories" begin, but here we are.

As the night wrapped up, our friendly neighborhood pimp walked me to my car (chivalry isn't dead, apparently). Now these were my *friends*. Well, except for the murder guy. I'd just met him that night, which, looking back, doesn't exactly make the story sound any better.

Earlier that same week, my drug-dealing ex-boyfriend decided he wasn't a fan of my new drug-dealing boyfriend. Naturally, he handled his emotions the mature way: by threatening to kill both of us.

Romantic.

In response, my new boyfriend invited all his gang member friends over to his house and everybody brought their guns. We sat there, waiting to see if my ex would show up. Thankfully, he never did.

During those years, I saw people get stabbed, I lost another ex to an overdose, and it was normal to lose friends and acquaintances to violent crimes.

One night, after a heated argument, an ex-boyfriend pulled out a gun, screaming that he was going to kill me. I don't know what made him change his mind, but instead of pointing it at me, he aimed at the ceiling and pulled the trigger. (Clearly, since I'm here writing this. #Winning)

I remember thinking, *Maybe there's something else out there for me. Something better than this?* But I didn't know because this was normal for where I was from, so I thought people generally lived like this everywhere.

Looking back, I've made more mistakes than I can count. I was lost and doing things that didn't serve me or anyone else. The idea that I'd one day build successful 7-figure businesses online feels almost unbelievable when I think about the past.

But here's the thing: no matter how much of a mess I was, I could always laugh at myself.

Oddly enough, that same humor is what eventually made my businesses take off.

At one point, I was living in the middle of nowhere, surrounded by farmland, with no Wi-Fi, no car, and a screaming newborn who looked at me like, *"Really, Mom? This is the plan?"* I was a newly single mom, completely overwhelmed, but instead of falling apart (well, maybe more like *after* falling apart), I started making silly videos on my cell phone.

I'd drive into town to find Wi-Fi, post those funny little videos online, and, to my surprise, those goofy clips made me more money than I ever did working my butt off at a "real" job.

They went viral and brought in millions of views and millions in sales for my products. Companies even started paying *me* to make funny ads for *their* businesses. (So cool.)

These days, entrepreneurs join my coaching programs to learn how to make entertaining content to bring in sales for their businesses too. I've also taught my methods on stages in multiple countries.

Looking back, every terrible experience came with a lesson. Those early days, sitting in clubs, drinking until I threw up, dealing with abusive boyfriends, weren't just random low points. They were the experiences that helped me figure out what I wanted, and most importantly, what I DIDN'T want.

This brings me to you. Now, I'm guessing you're not hanging out in strip clubs with drug dealers (and if you are, hey, no judgment! We all start somewhere). But maybe you're stuck in a situation that feels impossible. Maybe you're thinking there's no way out. I get it. I've been there. And I'm here to tell you that if I could turn my mess into a message, and then turn that message into millions? You can absolutely turn your situation around too.

In this book, I'm going to share how I built my own successful online business as a single mom. It's packed with stories that taught me incredible lessons and step-by-step tutorials to help you create funny videos that can bring in a buttload of sales for your business too.

Because if there's one thing I've learned, it's this: people love to laugh, and they also love to buy stuff while they're laughing.

WHO IS THIS BOOK FOR?

- Entrepreneurs in every niche! Whether you sell digital products, Physical products, coaching, live events, services, agency work, and more. This is for ALL businesses in EVERY category.
- Someone who's dreaming of starting an online business but feels totally lost (trust me, I've been there!)
- Someone who already has a business but wants to make it scale in a massive way with fun marketing that actually works
- Someone who likes learning through stories instead of boring lectures

If someone who started her journey surrounded by drug dealers and going through single motherhood can figure it out, I promise you can too. And yes, this really is the story of how I made my first million dollars with a toilet and a cell phone. (Don't worry, I'll explain.)

DUMB PRODUCTS THAT MADE PEOPLE RICH

There are so many dumb products that have made people rich. So it's interesting to me when entrepreneurs get stuck on asking themselves whether they are good enough, or whether their offer is also good enough to succeed in business.

Most people think they need to go to motivational events or listen to affirmations each day to believe in themselves enough to "make it." But do you know what should be enough to make you believe in your business? Looking at all the useless products out there that have made people millionaires. Think about it. If something as dumb as a Chia Pet can continuously make millions of dollars, what could you do with an actual product that has a real purpose?

Besides the Chia Pet, there is the Pet Rock, the Shake Weight, and more. These products don't exactly change lives, yet their creators made millions. Why? Because they make people laugh.

Take the Shake Weight. It's basically a goofy dumbbell that people thought was hilarious because it looked like someone was doing something phallic to an inanimate object. Google it! It even received millions of dollars' worth of free advertising when shows like *South Park* did parodies and skits about it. The creator went on *The Tonight Show* and so much more, completely free, because people couldn't stop laughing at it.

The Chia Pet was basically just grass in the shape of random things like a Scooby-Doo head because, apparently, that's what humanity needed.

The Pet Rock was literally a rock that does absolutely nothing.

Someone just walked by a rock and said, "You know what's better than a dog? A rock. Less poop. Let's sell it for $10."

Humor breaks all the rules. While others are out there trying to create the next big, life-changing thing, someone is flying around in a private jet because they put a rock in a box or made grass look like Donald Trump on a Chia Pet.

That got me thinking: *If a rock in a box can make millions, why not me?*

But here's the next big question. What happens when you take that same funny marketing strategy approach they did, but combine it with a product that actually solves a real problem? You get pure magic.

Look at Dollar Shave Club. They sold *razors*, which are not exactly hilarious. Their funny ads helped them sell the company for a BILLION dollars. Or what about Geico? They turned boring car insurance into a household name, all thanks to humor. When you combine funny marketing with an actual product or service that solves a real problem and brings even bigger value to the market-place? Now you could have a BILLION dollar company.

If you've got a product or service that brings value to the world, but you're holding back because you think the competition is too fierce or you're not "good enough," snap out of it.

Success isn't about having the perfect product or being the perfect person. It's about finding the right way to connect with people. And the best way to connect with people is through humor. And in my journey to seven figures, it all started in the most unlikely of places: my garage.

LIVING IN MY GARAGE
YOU CAN HATE YOUR LIFE AND STILL MAKE MONEY

After a breakup, I became a single, expecting mother. I was five months pregnant when my son's dad and I split up. As I drove from California to Las Vegas alone in a car full of my things, I could feel my son kicking. It wasn't exactly what I had on my vision board.

I pulled up to the garage where I would be living. Not the cute Pinterest kind with fairy lights and inspirational quotes. It was just your basic car hole. Except instead of a car, it would house me, my growing baby bump, and my crushed dreams. (Cue the world's worst version of "My Heart Will Go On" while you visualize all of this)

I had been a working musician, doing live performances to support myself. I was a pianist and singer, but with the weight gain from my pregnancy, I couldn't stand for more than a few minutes at a time. I had also had an accident. While walking into a gig at a casino one night, I slipped and fell, injuring my knees so badly I needed surgery. It's kinda hard to perform when you've blown up like a balloon, and your knees don't work. To make it worse, I looked exactly like The Penguin from the original *Batman* movie.

I guess I could have looked worse than an evil, unattractive, big-bellied, waddling penguin. I can't really think of anything that looks worse right now, but I'm sure there's something.

With my performing career temporarily limited, and an anticipation of medical bills and baby expenses coming up, I needed a place to live that matched my budget of approximately zero dollars. That's how I ended up in that garage and then eventually at Big Lots. I needed a couch that I could sleep on for my glamorous living arrangements. If you've never been to Big Lots, it's like Walmart, but way sketchier. You can buy a bed for cheap, and if you hang out in the parking lot long enough, you can buy drugs and also be pitched a good time with "Sally," who may or may not actually be a man.

It's a vibe.

Anyhow, for clarity, I had a home in Vegas that I couldn't afford to live in, so I rented out all the rooms on Airbnb to pay the mortgage. I slept in the garage and somehow managed to go unnoticed by the renters inside. Or maybe nobody said anything because they felt sorry for the sad pregnant lady in the garage who looked like the Penguin from *Batman* and cried herself to sleep every night.

This is a picture of my MTV Cribs-worthy accommodation.

But it was in that garage that I stumbled across something that would change my life. A friend handed me Russell Brunson's book *Expert Secrets*, and one thing hit me like a ton of bricks: if you know how to do something that others want to learn, you can teach others how to do it, and they'll pay you for it. AND you don't have to have a huge following to be able to make a million dollars.

For example, you can sell courses, books, coaching, and even physical products online. Basically, you can sell anything. And when you break down the math, I learned that if I make a course, for example, I could sell it for $997. And if just 1,000 people buy it? BOOM! That's a MILLION dollars.

This was the complete opposite of what I'd been hearing about needing a zillion followers and becoming a mega-influencer to make money online. I knew at least 1,000 people on this planet would want to learn what I had to offer!

See, I had built myself up to making $100k a year as an independent musician. I knew how to book tours on cruise ships, promote my music online, I had performed for crowds of up to 10,000 people, and I could show others how to make a living from music without a record label or manager. I was determined to coach others and to make a living doing music too!

Now, as much as I hated living in that garage, it was where I studied, built my first products that I sold online, and cried my eyes out in the breaks in between the work.

I remember when I sold my first course. (This was one of the many products I've sold online) I held my first webinar in that garage despite the loud noise of the water softener that turned on every few minutes. Sometimes, I had to scream into the computer so people could hear me because of it. I kept my camera off so they couldn't see the dark, depressing garage I called home, the convertible couch that I had bought from Big Lots, and the piece of makeshift carpet I had on the floor. The occasional cockroach was there as a gentle reminder of the bad decisions I had made in life. I had earned a good living as a musician, but a few bad life choices led me to not have much to show for it.

Over the next few months, my life would change dramatically in a way that I couldn't have expected. My situation as a single mother would force me to ask myself big questions like, *How can I build a million-dollar business with almost no time on my hands while raising a newborn? How do I sell stuff online even though I have no Wi-Fi and limited cell phone service? Why do I look like The Penguin from Batman while all these other pregnant chicks look super cute?*

These days, my life looks pretty different from when I was that pregnant penguin lady living in a garage. When I got my award for hitting my first million dollars in sales, I felt like Rocky at the end of the movie. You know, beaten up, totally exhausted, probably should've been in the hospital, but with my fists in the air yelling, "ADRIAN!"

That was just the start of many businesses I'd go on to build over the next few years. And all of it happened because I figured out how to make silly videos on my cell phone that SELL. And I figured it out while in a world where video content rules everything.

But here's the cool thing: sometimes your life has already given you exactly what you needed to succeed. You just might not know it yet. For me, growing up with a humble family that could find humor in absolutely anything had taught me something valuable: when you don't have a lot, every day is an adventure. It's like playing "How long will the electricity be shut off this month?" or "How many ways can we eat Spam?"

That million-dollar business I built with just a toilet and a cell phone? That story actually starts way before the garage, back when I was just a chubby kid nicknamed "Fatty," living in government housing, and learning that sometimes the best way to deal with life is to laugh at it.

THEY CALLED ME FATTY

When I was a kid, we lived in this house that the government paid for. We earned only $100 a week. When the heating was shut off, my mom would boil water on the stove so we could take warm baths. Back then, I thought rich people shopped at Target. I even promised myself that one day, I'd be able to afford those $30 jeans that the "rich people" at Target could buy.

My mom had always dreamed of playing the piano, but my grandparents were immigrants from Mexico and were very poor. But when I was a kid, my mom bought me an old piano. Many of the keys were missing or damaged, but I didn't know the difference. I fell in love with music and the thought of performing around the world.

When we moved to Roswell, New Mexico, my family bought a house we could barely afford. We weren't making enough money, so there was a point where my sister and brother had to go live with my grandparents because my parents couldn't afford to raise them anymore. I didn't realize we were struggling. My parents always said things like, "Your brother and sister are going away for an adventure," like they were off to explore the Amazon instead of being sent to Grandma's because we couldn't afford to feed them. And as a bonus, I was thrilled to get all the attention. Not exactly my proudest moment, but hey, I was eight.

One day, my parents saved enough to buy a video camera, the kind that takes those huge VHS tapes. My brother, sister, and I started recording funny videos and playing them back, laughing at ourselves. We had different characters, props, and even different sets. It was our favorite thing to do.

My family also always had a dry, sarcastic, and sometimes dark sense of humor. I remember when my grandma was dying, my dad used to call me and say, "Grandma died!" and then, after a pause, he would say, "Just kidding!" We would all laugh, comment about what terrible people we were, and then continue on with whatever we were talking about. We loved her. My family just always used humor to deal with whatever real pain was happening in our lives.

Entering my teens, I was a little on the chubby side, so my family nicknamed me "Fatty." For years, they didn't call me by my real name but instead by different variations of Fatty, Fat-stuff, Fatty McGee… endearing names like that. (My brother still calls me that to this day.)

After calling me every variation of Fatty in the book, my family decided it would be funny to upgrade to calling me "cow" every day. We lived in the middle of nowhere, surrounded by farmland, and when we drove by cows, my dad would honk and say, "Look, it's Kristi's family!"

Before you feel bad for me, let's be clear: I wasn't exactly innocent in the joke department myself. I make fun of sensitive topics within my own family all the time.

When my sister came out as gay, I made it my mission to remind her, jokingly, that she needed to pray the gay away or she was headed straight to hell. (That's not something I actually believe. And by the way, if this offends you, you might want to put this book down now because, trust me, it only goes downhill from here.)

At the time of this book, my mom has cancer, and I had been planning a year of traveling around the world, but I am not doing that anymore so that I can stay and help her out at home. I've made it a point to complain that she "ruined my travel plans" and asked, "Why couldn't she have gotten cancer later?" She laughs, I laugh, we all laugh. It's just who we are, and we know none of us mean anything we say…. that much.

That same sense of humor that came from my family ended up

in the videos that we made with that VHS recorder: dry, sarcastic, and making fun of painful situations. Nothing was off limits.

I had no idea then that this relentless ability to find humor in life, even in the messiest, most painful moments, would actually be the thing that would make my future videos SELL a buttload online. It is the secret sauce to going viral online, building my business, and, ultimately, taking care of the people I love. Turns out, laughter isn't just good for the soul, it's pretty great for business too.

DOOR-TO-DOOR SALES AND MY
FIRST LESSON IN PAID TRAFFIC

When I was 17, I was dating my first drug dealer (don't worry, there were more to follow) and recording songs I had written in his "studio" that he built out in his closet. When I finished a few tracks, I decided to get CDs printed. I had no idea how I would sell them. I didn't have a fan club or any radio play or anything. But I knew I had to get in front of people.

I remembered how people used to knock on our door to sell random things to my family, and I figured—why not do the same with my CDs?

My first album was called *Cry*, which was a direct reflection of my emo teenage years. The cover was a black and white picture of me crouching in a corner, looking like the last photo someone took of me before they murdered me.

I ordered the CDs, and once they arrived, I started going door-to-door to try to sell them. I sang on people's doorsteps and played piano in the living rooms of little old ladies who looked like they hadn't had a visitor in years. I got yelled at by angry homeowners, chased by dogs, and had doors slammed in my face. But for about every ten people who hated my guts, one person would say yes and give me $10. I learned that sales was a numbers game.

I had this car that didn't have a working heater, so in the winter, I would drive around with a gigantic bed comforter wrapped around me to keep from freezing. It was like 20 degrees outside. I would walk in the cold until my body felt numb. In the summers, it got so hot that there were times I was so thirsty I couldn't speak.

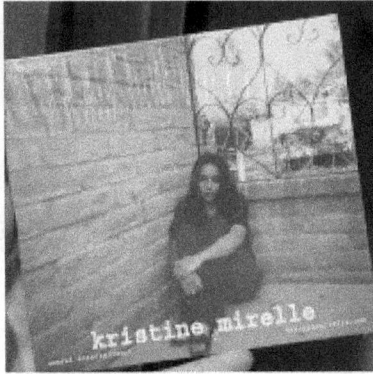

After doing door-to-door sales for a while, my dad suggested that I sell my CDs at the state fair. I paid for a booth for a few hundred bucks where I could set up and sell my album. I'd stand there, and pitch my CDs to every single person who walked by. I'd make a couple thousand working there for the week. Making $2,000–$2,500 in a week as an 18- or 19-year-old made me feel like I could do ANYTHING.

This taught me about paid traffic. I could make way more money faster by PAYING my way into places where traffic already existed. I also didn't have to walk in the blistering cold or crazy heat like when I went door to door.

I saw how if I paid to get in front of an already existing audience, where traffic already was, I could earn faster, and it was easier since traffic would come to me, and I didn't have to go to them.

The state fair had done the job of getting traffic to their venue, and now I was just paying to get quick access to THEIR audience that they worked so hard to build. I didn't have to spend years trying to build my own audience. I simply paid my way to get in front of theirs!

But there was a downside. Selling at the state fair meant standing on my feet for up to 8 hours a day. I had to be there in person, and it was exhausting. Sure, it was way better than going door to door, and I was making money faster thanks to the state fair's audience, but there was no way to grow this! There was only one of me, and I couldn't keep this up forever.

Even though I learned that paying to get in front of big audiences was a smart move, I realized there was a limit to how much I could make. My time and energy were running out, and I needed to find a better way to grow.

LESSONS LEARNED:

- *You can make your own products and then go out and sell them. (woohoo)*
- *You can sell directly to consumers by getting in front of them, like going door to door, but it's a crap ton of work.*
- *For even better results, you can pay to get quick access to other people's LARGER audiences to get sales faster and easier!*
- Although these were awesome discoveries, I learned that this was not scalable. I was physically worn out, and I had to search for a better way, so I kept asking bigger questions about how I could earn faster and easier.

I BECOME A PHONE SEX OPERATOR

I eventually moved to Hollywood, California. I was still struggling with money, and I ended up paying rent to sleep in someone's kitchen that I had found on Craiglist.com. (If you know anything about Craigslist, it's a site where you're equally likely to find a gig or a serial killer. If you know, you know) I would search Craigslist each day for random paying gigs and try to figure out how to pay the rent for my little cot next to my landlord's refrigerator. Going door to door wasn't always safe as a young female, so I had decided I wouldn't do that anymore.

Instead, I started doing this random depressing gig where I would get paid around $20/hour to basically be a phone-sex operator. It wasn't the best use of my time, but I needed to pay the rent, and shockingly, landlords don't accept "I'm chasing my dreams" as payment. So, for some time, my glamorous "music career" included this wonderful side gig.

After a while, I miraculously got my first paying music "gig." I was hired to play cover songs (songs by other famous artists) in a hotel in Hollywood. This is how I learned about how to get paid gigs even if you're not famous or have a huge following. Just find a venue with existing traffic (like hotel guests for example) and perform already well-known songs to their customers! The venue will want to pay you because you are providing value to their audience which in turn can help them earn more too. It's a very clear value exchange.

I was finally able to quit my glamorous sex operator job. Over the next eight years, that gig led to more gigs all over Beverly Hills, Malibu, and then contracts all over the world to exotic places like Tahiti, Bora Bora, Australia, Hawaii, and more. I was seeing the world because of music, but I worked incredibly hard. Sometimes, I would perform until 2 a.m. and have to be at the venue all day. I'd drive hours to a gig, or have to haul instruments, speakers, and mixing boards from venue to venue.

After years of performing on stage, I wanted something different. The days and nights were too long, and I was an alcoholic. There was a span where I drank every day for 32 days straight. I had between 5-10 drinks a day. I was constantly hungover, and would often fall asleep in parking lots of the venues where I was performing so I wouldn't drink and drive. (I mean, at least I was a *responsible* hot mess, right?)

During this time, I saw people online making money from their laptops, and I thought how amazing it would be to never have to *be* anywhere at any specific time and to work from wherever I wanted. I loved traveling and doing music, but I was drinking too much, and I was starting to feel like I wasn't a musician anymore, but more like one of those mechanical monkeys that you put a quarter in, and they dance or do whatever you want them to do on stage. I knew it was time for a change.

I GET MY FIRST SALES (AND GET BANNED FROM CRAIGSLIST)

A s I mentioned previously, I found out I was pregnant, and at about 5 months, my relationship ended, and I packed up my life in Los Angeles. I drove to Las Vegas to my new "home" in a garage. Not exactly the dream setup for bringing a baby into the world, but there I was.

I needed to start earning fast, but when I first started, I had nothing to sell. I knew how to book paid gigs as a musician, and I knew there were tons of musicians who would also love to learn how. So I thought about creating a course teaching this exact thing, but I knew that would take a while to finish. Because I needed to start earning as quickly as possible, I decided to offer one-on-one coaching since I could start immediately.

My perfect customers were singers who loved to sing cover songs and, ideally, were already actively singing, at least at home. Cover songs are basically songs sung by other people. Think "Brown Eyed Girl" by Van Morrison, "Free Fallin'" by Tom Petty, or modern music by artists like Ed Sheeran, Beyoncé, or anyone recognizable.

Like the lesson I had learned when I got hired to perform at the hotel in Hollywood, there are places like casinos, bars, hotels, and restaurants that already have audiences and need entertainment to keep them there. These venues will pay artists to play familiar songs that keep guests happy and spending money, like at the bar.

This means you can get paid to perform, even without a fan base or a hit song, because the venue is making money.That's exactly how I traveled to places like Bora Bora, Tahiti, Australia, and all over the U.S., getting paid to perform on stages, even though I wasn't famous.

I asked myself how I could get in front of my ideal customer, someone with the talent and desire to sing for a living. Those would be my ideal coaching clients.

First, I started reaching out to singers directly on social media. In fact, it reminded me a lot of my "door-to-door" sales days, except that it was all digital, and I didn't have to worry about getting chased by someone's dog or being mistaken for a Jehovah's Witness.

I sent tons of private messages to musicians and set up phone calls individually. Sometimes, I'd spend the entire day on sales calls. I pitched my one-on-one coaching and told them that I would work with them personally to get results. I wanted testimonials and proof that my system worked, so I put a lot of extra effort into getting them going. I spent my entire days reaching out to people, on sales calls, and private messaging people.

Then I remembered a lesson from the state fair: if I *paid* to get in front of my audience, I'd get faster results. So I posted ads on Craigslist.com in their "gigs available" section for $5 in each city. (Wasn't much, but it worked enough!)

That's when I was reminded of such a valuable lesson. Because I PAID to get my offer in front of other people on a larger scale, I didn't have to chase people on social media anymore. Instead, *they* were coming to *me*. It made my life so much easier. Now I spent my day responding to people who wanted what I had to offer! I wasn't begging people to talk to me. They were reaching out first, and let me tell you, that made a HUGE difference!

I got sales faster and easier since the leads were better. I sold my first few coaching programs, and my students started getting results. They were booking paid gigs everywhere. Many of them had never played a paid show in their lives before working with me, and I was ecstatic.

But within just a few weeks, Craigslist banned me. They said my ads went against their guidelines, so I needed to come up with a different solution.

I needed to find a new platform to pay to get in front of my audience. But while I was figuring that out, I heard about something called affiliate marketing, something I had never heard of before.

Here's how it works: people who *already* have an audience can promote your product for free. You don't pay them upfront. You just split the profits if someone purchases. And if no sales happen, no one owes anyone anything.

For someone like me, with no email list and no followers, I was about to learn something super valuable!

LESSONS LEARNED:

- *You can reach out directly to people on social media to get sales even if you have no audience, but this takes a lot of time and effort.*
- *Paying to fast-track your way to get in front of larger audiences means you can get more sales faster. I started out with Craigslist, but there are other methods that I will discuss in the following chapters.*

HOW TO GET SALES WITHOUT A FOLLOWING

At this time, I was still living in Las Vegas in my garage, and I continued performing gigs occasionally here and there, but I had gained so much weight at this point from my pregnancy that it was painful to sit at a piano.

I kept asking myself, *How can I sell more without working more?* I decided I would create my first webinar. I mentioned it before, but if you don't know what it is, it's where you can get a bunch of people to log onto a group video call, teach them something valuable, or offer a demonstration of your products and services. At the end, you offer something that they can buy. This is way better than doing one-on-one sales because in a webinar, instead of selling just to one person, you can sell to hundreds or even thousands of people all at once.

I poured all my energy into building my first webinar presentation and even finally finished creating my first course to go with it. In the webinar, I taught "How to Book a Gig in 7 Days." I showed artists exactly how to find venues with budgets to pay performers. I knew there were tons of artists whose lives could be changed for the better by what I was going to share. At the end, I would sell my course that would give them even more thorough step-by-step guidance.

The problem was I had no email list, no followers, and no traffic.

So I asked myself, *How do I sell my course if nobody knows it even exists?*

This is a problem that most online business owners have. It's not that they don't have a good offer; it's that they have no idea how to get their business in front of their ideal customers!

That was when I learned about something called "affiliate partnerships." The concept is, if you have an offer, figure out who your ideal customers are, and then go find other people who already have your audience. Ask them if they will promote your products, services, or whatever you sell, and then split the income with them 50/50.

I immediately asked myself, *Who has my same audience (musicians) that might want to buy my course on how to book gigs?*

Vocal coaches! Vocal coaches teach people how to sing, and I figured a large percentage of the singers they teach would also want to perform on stage and get paid for it!

I immediately went to YouTube and started reaching out to every vocal coach I could find who had a decent number of views on their videos. I asked if they had an email list and if they would be interested in selling my course, and we could split the revenue.

I probably reached out to 100 influencers, schools, and vocal coaches before one agreed to promote my webinar.

The vocal coach sent out a few emails inviting his followers to my webinar (I wrote the emails for him so that he didn't have to do any work), and the following week, I taught my first webinar to his audience. I was too scared to do the first webinar live, so I pre-recorded it and then played it for the live audience. (I was such a sissy for doing that.) I was still living in the garage at the time, and I didn't want to do it live on video. I figured people might question buying something from someone who looks like they live in the storage department of Home Depot.

Now, when I finally did get the courage to do my first LIVE webinar, the Wi-Fi was awful in my garage. I lost connection three times, and the screen went black for what felt like an eternity. But, like any good disaster, I powered through the chaos, and people stuck around. I was teaching something that could change their lives, and they were excited to learn more! I pitched my course at the end of the training, and crossed my fingers that we would get sales.

It worked. My affiliate and I made almost $5,000 in a few days, which we split 50/50. I couldn't believe it. I had actually cracked the code on how to get customers quickly even though I had no audience.

Find businesses that serve your same audience, and ask them to promote your offer. Split the revenue, and it becomes a win-win for everybody. This is how you get FREE traffic.

It was great because I got to tap into his audience, and he didn't have to lift a finger to sell or deal with any of the fulfillment. I handled all of that. It was the perfect partnership where everyone walked away happy.

I want you to understand something incredibly valuable about this. You are basically getting FREE traffic in this type of situation. You don't have to pay, post a ton online, or spend years building an audience. You just tap into someone else's already existing audience by providing value that compliments their business.

Finding affiliates is one way to bring in leads and sales for your business, even if you have no existing audience. It does take time and a lot of hustle, but it's worth the work! But what I didn't realize at the time was that I was about to stumble upon another solution that would explode my business practically overnight… and it was just around the corner.

LESSONS LEARNED:

- *You can get sales quickly by finding another person or business that already has a following of your ideal customers. Ask them to promote your offer, and split the revenue. This is how you get FREE traffic and can save years of time.*
- *In this chapter, I shared how I used a webinar to sell my course but you can do joint-promotions selling ANYTHING.*

- *Here's the truth: most affiliates will either say no or won't respond at all. It's normal. This process takes time, patience, and a lot of follow-ups. But don't get discouraged. You don't need hundreds of affiliates. Just a few people saying yes can make a huge impact on your business. Keep going!*

MY SON ARRIVES!

A few months before my son was born, I finally moved out of that grimy garage into a real bedroom and started to prepare for his birth.

At around eight months, I went in for an exam, only to find out I needed an emergency C-section. I'll be honest: staring down at my belly and knowing they were about to cut my stomach in half and pull my baby out of me wasn't exactly my idea of how to spend a Wednesday night.

The surgery was a success, and after he was born, I realized that raising a baby is like running a 24/7 daycare for a tiny dictator who never sleeps. London (my son) cried all the time, didn't seem to like me, and left me so sleep-deprived that I honestly thought I might die. I'd sit in a rocking chair all night, holding him while my neck screamed in pain. My nipples would bleed from breastfeeding, and I was so paranoid about smothering him that I stayed awake the entire time he nursed.

Fun times.

Each week, I would scrape up whatever was left of my soul and go teach my webinar and pitch my course on how to book shows for aspiring musicians. My sibling was a God-send, and would help watch my son during those hours. I still didn't really have an audience or much of an email list, but I would get an affiliate every now and then to promote it. I got enough sales to keep me motivated but not enough to feel entirely secure.

I was still making sales by cold-messaging random musicians on social media, but after a few months of my son crying non-stop, I had to quit. Turns out, yelling, "SORRY, MY BABY IS SCREAMING! DO YOU WANT THE COURSE OR NOT?" doesn't exactly close the deal.

With my son's arrival, I knew I needed a better solution. I needed something that worked for *my* life as a new mom, without having to juggle sales calls during nap time (or tantrum time). So, I kept searching for a way to build my business that fit my reality.

HOW I BUILT A MONEY-MAKING MACHINE WITH ONE HAND AND A BREAST PUMP

L ife with a newborn meant I needed a change. After performing 2,500 shows in my career, singing at smoky casinos until 2 a.m., I had lived out my dreams of making a living as a musician and was ready to "retire." Instead, I wanted to coach musicians full-time and help them live out their musical dreams.

That's when I decided I would write a book.

This is a picture of me holding my son while I worked on my first book. I would hold him with one arm (I was also breastfeeding at the time), and with my other hand, I would write very, very slowly since I didn't have the use of both hands. But progress is better than no progress.

The book was a list of Festivals that paid artists to perform. Each festival had confirmed budgets all around the country, so it was an incredible resource for artists who loved the idea of performing for a living! I included tutorials like how to contact the agents, what to send them, and how to put together a winning show. I gave them everything they needed to know to book paid shows.

Once I finished creating it, I asked myself again, *But how am I actually going to sell this?* That whole idea of *"if you build it, they will come"* is a big pile of nonsense. How can people buy from you if they don't even know you exist?

I realized I had to do what worked for me before. I needed to pay to get in front of the right audience and then let my customers come to me. Just like I paid for booths at the state fair to reach people who were already there, or how I paid for Craigslist ads to sell my courses, I knew I had to invest in getting in front of my ideal customers if I wanted results quickly and at a bigger scale.

I didn't have time or energy to post daily or go live all the time while raising a newborn. So, I thought, "What if I make *one* video, run it as an ad, and let it work for me?"

This question changed my life.

One day during my son's nap time, I grabbed my cell phone and decided it was time to make my first video and tell the world about my book! My cheeks looked like they were melting off of my face. My voice was also so shot that I sounded like a chain smoker, but I powered through. "I'm going to show you how to book fun shows at fairs and festivals!" I rasped, trying to squeeze in my pitch before my son woke up from his nap.

I took that janky cell phone video, and I hired a guy for $300 online to run ads for me. They started running on Facebook and Instagram, and sales started coming in immediately. I didn't have a lot of money, so I only spent around $60 the first day, but I made like $100. Then, I would take the small profit I made and reinvest it right back into running more ads the next day. When I spent $100, I made $200. Then, the next day, I spent $200, made $350, and so on. I kept spending as long as I was earning more than what I was spending.

My mind was blown. There was a glimpse of light at the end of the tunnel. I didn't have to message musicians all day on social media and try to find traffic. I didn't have to post all day, either. Instead, I just made one video, ran it as an ad, put a little money behind it, and it was working for me and earning me money while I was doing mom duties.

At the time, I was still performing at local casinos and piano bars, but I could see sales coming in on my phone during my breaks.

I was also still breastfeeding at the time and would pump milk in the bathroom stalls or storage units backstage during my breaks. I would pull out my breast milk pumps and sit there pumping milk while staring at my phone and watching sales come in.

After I was done, I'd walk back down the casino lobbies and onto the stage with the milk in hand. I kept a bucket of ice next to my piano, and that's where I would put the precious bottles of milk to keep them cold so I could give them to my son when I returned home after my gigs.

Imagine a woman on stage with milk leaking out of her nipples while she's dancing around on stage singing "Uptown Funk." It's kinda hilarious and depressing at the same time.

But what was happening simultaneously was miraculous. I had made the single best discovery of my life: how to make money on autopilot and how to earn even while I was doing other things. I would wake up to discover that I earned more money while sleeping than I did while working. I discovered "paid marketing," how to create ads, and even what to say in my videos that made people WANT TO BUY. I felt important. I felt like I had something to offer the world. People were telling me about how they were getting results in their music careers and how I was making a difference and changing their lives. I was providing for my son. It was awesome.

Once again, I didn't post every day. I didn't spend hours creating content, and I didn't even go live. I created an ad *once*, and it didn't require a ton of time, energy, or any fancy equipment. I had a great product and paid ads helped bring people TO ME instead of me chasing THEM. It would bring in sales on auto-pilot. I was profiting about $300 a day at the time when I first made this discovery.

As I mentioned before, my first ad was simple and nothing special.

Scan the QR code with your phone to take a look!

SCAN ME

If you've watched it, you're probably thinking how unimpressive it is. And you're absolutely right. But that's exactly the point. If my simple, imperfect ad could bring in money while I slept, imagine what YOU could do.

Later on, I would start to make the biggest discovery of my life: how to make FUNNY ads that would completely EXPLODE my business. We will get there, but in the meantime, you first need to learn how to make ads that SELL and what to SAY in your ads to get customers to throw money at you, even if your ad is made on a janky little cell phone.

- Step 1 is to make ads that sell.
- Step 2 is to make *those* ads funny to really put gasoline on the fire.

So first, let's start with Step 1 in the next chapter!

LESSONS LEARNED:

Make an Irresistible Offer: Find something your audience can't resist that saves them time and/or money.

- *Build a site where people can buy from you!*
- *Keep Testing: Create different products, services, and more to see which ones work!*
- *VIDEOS ARE THE BEST WAY TO PROMOTE YOUR PRODUCTS:*
- *Invest in Ads: Don't be afraid to spend money to get your videos in front of the right audience. Ads are the BEST way to scale your business.*

MAKE PEOPLE THROW MONEY
AT YOU

Ever wonder why people buy headache medicine? Simple: their head hurts! Obvious right? But this simple idea is the *magic key* to connecting with your customer. What's their biggest challenge? What keeps them tossing and turning at night? What problem are they desperate to solve? If you can clearly show them that you have the solution, they'll want to *click* your video and buy what you have to offer!

That's the whole goal of advertising: attracting the customer with the problem your product solves and making them realize just how friggin' awesome your solution is.

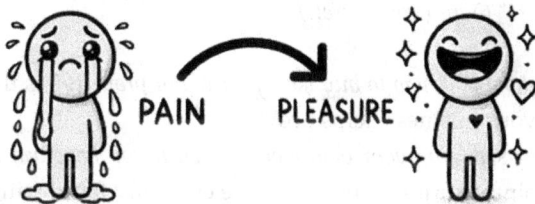

To create videos that *SELL LIKE CRAZY*, remember this: your customer wants to go away from pain and towards pleasure.

It's like this: when you have a headache, you don't care about fancy scientific words or how many lab coats the scientists wore while making the medicine. You just want the headache gone. Your customers are the same way.

Ask yourself two questions:

- What pain point are you taking your ideal customer *away* from?
- What are the *benefits and results or pleasure* your product/services provide?

Many ads miss these important points. I frequently see failing ads that focus on stuff nobody cares about. For example, if you have a real estate investing course, you wouldn't want to start your ad by saying, "I'll show you how to measure door frames and provide 30 hours of content for you to watch."

Nobody cares. In fact, when you make your videos, you should always do the "Nobody Cares Test."

- *Example: Real Estate Course: "My course has 18 modules and 500 videos."*

(Does anybody care? Nope. Nobody cares.)

- *Example 2: "I'll show you how to buy your first property without spending your own money, even if you have bad credit!" (Yep! People care!!)*

"I will show you how to buy your first rental property" is the benefit *and* result your business helps provide.

"Without spending your own money, even if you have bad credit," is the pain point your ideal customers are currently faced with.

See what we did there? We addressed their pain point and offered a solution all in one sentence. That's what hooks your customer.

Think of it like this: If you were starving and someone offered you pizza, would you care about who invented pizza dough or how long it took to bake? Nope! You just want to know it's hot, cheesy, and ready to eat RIGHT NOW!

But here's the problem: too many businesses write long, boring stories about their history in their ads. Like we did previously, let's do the "nobody cares" test. When you're hungry, do you care more about whether the pizza is delicious or whether **the tomatoes were picked by a guy named Bob, who's been farming since 1973?** Exactly.

Now, I'm not saying a good story isn't valuable or that people don't care about supporting good businesses. But in an ad where you've got only 15 seconds to catch someone's attention, starting with "Back when I was a kid..." usually isn't the best way to get the most sales. Keep it short, sweet, and straight to the point of what's in it for the customer!

One easy way to create messaging that sells is to fill out this sentence.

I'll show you how to [DESIRED RESULT] without [PAIN POINTS].

Let's go back to our real estate example. What keeps potential real estate investors staring at the ceiling at 3 a.m.? What are the pain points they currently want to solve?

Examples are:

- They hate their soul-crushing 9-5 job
- That nightmare boss
- Only being able to afford one vacation a year (to their in-laws' house... yay!)
- Missing their kid's baseball game for the millionth time

In your video ad, you need to focus on THAT! Let them know your products and services solve those problems that they think about night and day. Not that it comes with a 99-page PDF.

One of my students teaches parents of autistic children how to help their kids speak faster. Her original messaging? A detailed explanation of the six *facial muscle groups that kids need to be able to control to be able to speak.* While fascinating, it missed the mark because no parent wakes up thinking, *Wow, I really wish I understood facial muscle mechanics today!*

What do parents with autistic children want?

For their child to say their first words. For their children to be able to communicate with their friends and family and have a better quality of life.

We changed her messaging so that it focused only on the result!

- "Is your autistic child struggling to speak? What if I could show you three simple steps to help them say their first words, sometimes YEARS FASTER."

Is your autistic child struggling to speak?- hits their pain point

Help them start talking sometimes years faster- is the result they could get!

The difference? Night and day. Parents immediately understand how her program solves their problem and gets them closer to that desired result they want so badly!

Here's the thing: selling isn't just about making money. When you learn to sell effectively, you're actually helping people achieve their dreams.

- That autistic child might say "I love you" for the first time.
- That frustrated employee might finally quit their soul-crushing job.
- That shower singer might end up performing on real stages. (I've seen it happen!)

One of my mentors said, "If you have something that can genuinely help people, you don't just have the right to sell it, you have an ethical obligation to get it out there!"

Your customer wants to go away from pain and towards pleasure.
If you can communicate that effectively in your ads,
you can generate a buttload of sales 🛡️

Here's the real secret sauce: People don't care about all the fancy features and complicated details. Focus on the pain point you solve and the result they desire!

In my videos for my music products, I say things like, "Are you tired of posting videos endlessly online waiting around for someone to discover you? *(pain point)* Do you want to make money performing on stages independently, even if you don't have a record label or manager? *(result they desire)* If you'd like to learn how you can travel the world, meet new people, build your fan base, and finally get your music heard, listen up! *(How I can help them)* " Then I would continue talking about my products and more about the pain points I help them solve!

Our main goal is to get them to *click* your video and create a desire for them to want to buy! The best way to do that? Show them exactly what's in it for them, and make it crystal clear why they *need* what you're offering.

Quick Checklist for Your Videos:

- What pain point are you solving? (Make it crystal clear!)
- What amazing result can you help your customers achieve? (Make it exciting!)
- Are you boring people with unnecessary details? (Stop that!)
- Are you giving them hope for a better future? (Do more of that!)

MY ARM-PITS GO VIRAL AND THE WORLD SHUTS DOWN

I was really excited that I was profitable. It was a dream, especially since I was doing very little work for it. Most of my day went to taking care of my newborn, so it was a Godsend for where I was at that time in my life.

One day, I was asking some friends for ideas on what I should do for my next ad. I had been making some pretty basic ads with me talking to the camera and had been doing just fine, but I knew there had to be more. My friend randomly said, "Why don't you hang upside down while standing on a tree?" I don't think he was serious, but I was immediately in. We walked across the street to the neighborhood park and found a tree. I'm not in shape, so it was extremely hard. It was 117 degrees outside, and I was sweating up a storm with noticeably sweaty armpits. I didn't really care. I was too exhausted to care. Too broke to care. And if there was any chance that I might be able to walk away from pumping breast milk in a public restroom in a casino, I was willing to do anything. I stood upside down against a tree and talked about my books for musicians. Once again, I shot everything on my cell phone: low quality, unscripted, and all.

I opened the ad, upside down, visibly sweaty armpits, and said, "You don't have to stand upside down on a tree just to get attention!!" and then continued telling musicians that they could get their music published online instead! My friend also said that experts usually end their ads on a "whiteboard" where they teach something. So, in my ad, I ended up at a whiteboard where I explained a little bit more about why these musicians would benefit from this book and a little bit more about how artists could promote their music. I had a splitting migraine, probably from the heat, the blood rushing to my head, and overly exerting myself to keep from falling on my head. I also didn't have mics, so I had to scream for the phone to pick up my audio.

But I'd do it all over again.

Because the next thing I knew, sales took off. Comments took off. People were watching, commenting, and sharing. Some people loved it. Some people hated it. It was just all part of the territory.

The next thing I knew, my quirky little ad brought in tons of sales! And you know what? Those wet armpits were making me more than before. Turns out being yourself, even if you're awkward and sweaty, is way more interesting than trying to be some polished "business expert."

I quickly learned that my "hook" (me standing upside down) caught the attention of viewers, which made people watch longer! This made people more interested in what I was selling because I had their eyes on my product!

I learned that trying to be serious like everyone else got me nowhere. Not only did it not sell as much, but it was boring, and I hated it. Standing upside down was way more fun. On set, we all laughed, joked, and had a good time. This was making business way more entertaining for myself and my customers.

To see the
"Upside Down on a Tree"
video
scan the QR code.

SCAN ME

I learned that trying to be serious online got me nowhere. Not only did it not sell as much, but it was boring, and I hated it.

My sales didn't just grow. They skyrocketed! In fact, they more than doubled what I was making before. And here's the wild part: when I ran a boring "normal" ad, it actually cost me *twice as much* to make a sale!

That's when it hit me. All those goofy little videos my siblings and I used to make as kids? Now I could make them as an adult... but actually get paid for it! All I had to do was sell something at the end. It felt like I had cracked the code.

Eventually, my son started daycare, which gave me a few precious hours during the day to focus on my business. Most nights, I'd still perform at the casinos to bring in extra income, and I kept selling the books I'd poured my heart into. Everything was clicking into place. I was still exhausted from being up all night with my newborn, but at least I was seeing progress.

But then something completely unexpected happened. We got word of a little thing called COVID, a virus that was spreading all over the world. And overnight, everything shut down. People were advised to stay in their homes. All my gigs were canceled, and the main source of how I was earning disappeared. Nobody wanted to buy a book about booking shows anymore when all the shows in the world weren't happening anymore. My son's daycare shut down, so I had nobody to watch him during the day. I was scared. There were riots going on around the country, and everything seemed so unsafe. I was too exhausted to continue on in my current state with no sleep and trying to build my business. There was one night when I held my son and fell to the ground because I was so tired. Luckily, he was fine, but I realized I needed help.

Within a few days, I was on a plane to move to Roswell, NM, to get help from my parents. The problem was they lived in the middle of nowhere, surrounded by farmland, and there was no steady Wi-Fi and very little cell phone service. How could I continue to build an online business without Wi-Fi?

HOW TO WRITE A HOOK THAT SELLS

Now that we talked about the importance of having a great hook, let's talk about one easy way to create a great hook for *your* business.

Quick reminder, the first few seconds of your video ad? That's your "hook." It's the most important part of your video because it is the biggest determining factor as to whether someone is going to choose to watch the rest of it. It's called "the hook" because we want to hook the viewers, grab their attention, and make them *want* to watch us talk about what we are selling.

Keep in mind that our ads are interrupting their day. Nobody woke up today and said, "I hope I see some ads today! That would be so much fun!" They're on social media because they want to be entertained. So it makes sense to create an ad that entertains them. The rest of our ad could be about an amazing product, but if they scroll away after just a few seconds, they'll never even see what you're selling.

Remember that your videos are competing with the most ridiculous videos, skits, and news articles in people's feeds. You're in the feed right between "Kim Kardashian is actually an octopus!" and "There's a comet heading for Earth, and we're all going to die!" We want to create something that can compete for people's attention.

One of the easiest ways to stop someone mid-scroll is to VISU-ALLY stand out. Not everyone watches with sound on, but they're always looking. So, think of your visuals as your first impression and make it count.

Here are some ideas to create scroll-stopping visual hooks:

- **Do Something Unexpected:** In my previous example, I stood upside down on a tree (not recommended after Taco Tuesday). You don't have to be a gymnast to pull this off. Even hilariously failing at something can be entertaining and make people pause to watch. Can you do a cartwheel? Ride a bike? Drive up in a tiny Hot Wheels car you're *waaaaay* too big for?
- **Pick a Fun Location:** I once filmed in front of a dairy farm and made cheesy cow puns like "Promote your mooo-sic!" Was it over the top? Yes. But it worked. You don't have to be cheesy (unless you want to), but do something at an interesting location that makes people think, *What's going on here?*
- **Use unique props and costumes.** I will be explaining more about how I create characters in a future chapter, but I want to note how awesome wearing a costume can be! I've ordered costumes from Amazon and dressed up as a cow, an elderly woman, a military sergeant, a ninja, and so much more! When I spoke at Funnel Hacking Live for the first time in 2022, I shared a funny idea for a fun video. I suggested that someone buy a pickle costume and then have their opening line be "In a pickle?" Basically, this line could serve any business! It could be referring to not having your taxes organized, forgetting your wife's anniversary, or doing a home repair gone bad.

Months later, someone let me know they actually dressed up as a pickle, and they said it was the best-performing ad they'd ever put out. Costumes and props don't just make your ad funny. They make it *memorable*. If someone scrolls away, there's a 0% chance they'll buy. So, go all in. Grab a silly hat, pull out a wacky prop, or stand in a weird location. Make people stop and think, *I need to see where this is going.*

WHEN LIFE HANDS YOU A TOILET, MAKE AN AD

Moving from Las Vegas to my parent's house in the middle of nowhere was like moving to a different dimension. I had no car and almost no connection to the outside world. I was only occasionally able to stream a few seconds of a video or read an article online about all the riots that were happening, how people were dying from COVID, and to watch as cars were on fire in my old neighborhood in Hollywood.

I was thankful that I moved to a place where my biggest fear was getting run over by a tractor, but the isolation in the middle of nowhere drove me crazy and made it challenging to try and grow an online business.

I couldn't do anything live online because I had almost no Wi-Fi. I couldn't do webinars, coaching, one-on-one consultations, sales calls, or anything that a digital entrepreneur could normally do to earn money. I was also still only getting a couple hours of sleep at night with my newborn.

But here's the thing: Sometimes, when you have few options, it can actually be a good thing. Now you are able to focus on ONE THING. I truly believe that was a blessing!

You know when you're in a plane, and you're flying over crop circles, desolate land, and then you see a few random houses in the middle of nowhere, and you wonder, *What kind of weirdos live there?* Yeah, that was where I was living. I had worse than dial-up-internet quality, no car, and barely one bar of cell phone service if I stood at specific locations around our home.

The book that I had been selling was specifically about how to book paid shows. As I mentioned before, now that all the shows were canceled due to COVID, nobody wanted to learn about how to book shows. I turned off all my ads and went back to square one. I needed to figure out a new product I could sell.

This is where many entrepreneurs stop. They find something that works, and when it stops working, they think that's it! Their career is over, and there's no other alternative. Or worse, they blame the world and take on a victim mentality because it's just easier that way than to take responsibility for figuring out what to do next.

But there's always a solution to every problem, and honestly, I don't even like to call it a problem. I prefer the word "opportunity." You never know what you'll find when you keep going!

When COVID hit and I found myself stuck on that farm, my book about booking live shows became completely irrelevant overnight. With every gig in the world canceled, I had to adapt.

I decided on two things:

1. I'd write a new book tailored to the current reality for musicians. I would teach them how to promote their music online.
2. I'd create better, more engaging ads to connect with my audience and sell it.

Here's the truth: as a business owner, you should expect that what works today might not work tomorrow. That's just how it goes. And it's okay! The key is to embrace the challenge, pivot when needed, and keep pushing forward. Success isn't about never hitting roadblocks. It's about learning to climb over them, go around them, or knock them down altogether. Just don't stop working to figure it out.

First, I worked on my new book about how musicians could promote their music from home. They could use the internet to get their music published on various media outlets, all from their laptops! It was something I had done dozens of times, so it was easy for me to share tutorials. Since we were all on lockdown during the pandemic, this would be super helpful to musicians with the new restrictions we had!

I did research and created a list of blogs, magazines, podcasts, and other outlets that were actively seeking independent musicians to cover! I included all of their available contact information. It took hundreds of hours to compile the list, but that's why it would be so valuable to artists! I would save them a ton of time and then give them free bonus tutorials on how to use it.

Once my product was ready, I sat down to write my very first ad to promote my book. Now, let me be clear: I still didn't have a team, a videographer, fancy writers, or some big Hollywood studio to film in. I just worked with what I had.

If you're in a position to invest more money into fancy equipment and a team, GREAT! If not, that's ok too! I started out with very little and earned multiple seven figures in sales with just videos from my cell phone.

So, I looked around and took stock of my *resources*. In the backyard, there was a toilet, some oranges, a plastic horse, a stack of children's books, and a lawnmower. Oh, and my brother and his girlfriend happened to be hanging around that day. Perfect! I had all the props, locations, and "actors" I needed to make my ad.

Now, I know some of you are wondering why we had a toilet in our backyard. Well, a few weeks earlier, my mom's toilet had given up on life, so naturally, we replaced it ourselves. Because, you know, when you're Mexican, you're automatically a plumber, landscaper, and a general handyman, even if you have zero idea what you're doing. We genuinely believe we can do it just as well as the pro we didn't want to pay. We always convince ourselves it's worth the $20 we saved, even if the results are questionable.

When we replaced our toilet, we just put the old toilet in the backyard like any traditional Latino family would do, right next to the old washing machine and dryer that we never threw away either.

I asked my brother if he would sit on the toilet and his girlfriend if she would film the ad with my cell phone. I considered a couple of things:

- What kind of "hook" should we create?
- How could I entertain my audience during the entire ad?
- How could I communicate to my audience what pain point my product solves?
- How could I use each of the props?
- What should I write on the whiteboard?

I decided to use the horse in the opening shot, juggle the oranges, have my brother sit on the toilet, and then end up at the whiteboard doing something silly.

It was time to shoot the ad. My son was outside crying in his little walker. I wheeled my wailing baby into the laundry room. I promised him I would get this done in three takes and that I would be right back. At this time, he wasn't even one year old yet, so he didn't understand a thing I said, and I felt super guilty wheeling him into the laundry room since he was screaming his head off. Unfortunately, having a screaming baby in the background of an ad probably wouldn't have converted well, so I didn't have much of a choice.

Also, there was a tornado touching down about a mile in front of our house. We could see it from where we were filming, and it was starting to get windy. We would have only a few shots before we needed to go inside. My mom was pleading for us to run in and take shelter.

I quickly sat on a rocking horse, juggled the oranges, pushed that lawnmower, and spoke some ridiculous Spanish. Then I ended up chatting with "Harry" (my brother), who was buried in a newspaper, pretending to be a musician spending too much time on the toilet rather than promoting his music. I managed to talk about my new book and thankfully nailed it in just a couple of takes. I dressed extra cute and gave it my all.

After we were done, we quickly packed up everything and ran inside just before the wind arrive, and the rain started pouring outside.

I spent the next day editing it on my computer in between taking care of my little one. I manually added captions (no apps existed back then) and was ready to send it off to the world. (Note: Always add captions! Many people are scrolling social media without their sound on!)

I waited until my mom returned home so I could borrow her car to drive miles into town where there was Wi-Fi so I could upload the new ad. We didn't have Wi-Fi that was strong enough to be able to upload the ad at home, so I found a few spots in town where I could borrow the Wi-Fi to continue building my business.

I'll be honest; I didn't really have any big expectations. I thought the ad was good, but I didn't think it was anything special. I thought it was somewhat creative, but I wasn't really expecting a whole lot.

I sent it to the guy who ran my ads and just prayed to little baby Jesus that it would bring in some sales. I knew it was an awesome book, and I knew that what I was teaching could help musicians all over the world. I believed in the product, so I was just hoping the ad would successfully get eyes on it!

I couldn't have ever guessed what this one single video was going to do not just for my book, but for the rest of my life.

Overnight, the new ad *took off*, and sales of my new book soared. It racked up millions of views, I was getting hundreds of messages a day, and testimonials came flooding in from musicians who were getting their music published all around the globe. People were saying things like, "This is the best ad ever" and "This is the only ad that matters." Below are some of the fun comments I would get daily. How cool is it knowing that people *like* seeing your ads and are buying what you created? Normally, people *hate* ads. They change the channel; they scroll away. But now people were saying they couldn't wait to see my next one.

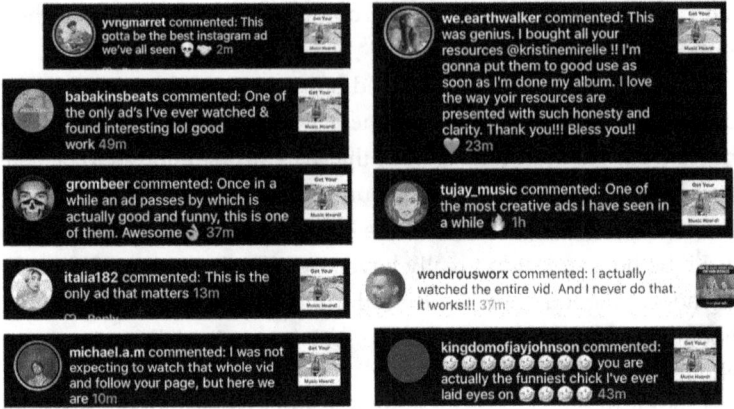

I was getting tons of followers on my social media accounts. My email list was growing substantially, I was making more and more money, and people were commenting about my brother "Harry" and how much they loved him, too. It was unlike anything I had ever experienced. How could one ad generate this much love from strangers? I learned that a great, entertaining ad doesn't just generate sales. It creates TRUST and LIKABILITY from your customers in a way that I've never witnessed.

People who weren't even musicians were commenting things like, "I'm not even a musician, and I want to buy her products!" *That was wild!*

I was just trying to get attention to my product, but I realized when you make someone laugh, it creates a whole new association. That person now associates YOU with those good feelings they got when they watched the ad. If consumers like to buy from companies they know, like, and trust, HUMOR is a fast track to get them there!

Scan the QR code with your phone to watch my "Toilet" Ad.

SCAN ME

After racking up millions of views, clicks, and shares, and making more SALES than ever, I realized one thing: **funny, entertaining ads were the secret sauce to blowing up my business.**

When I dug into the numbers, I was shocked. I hadn't changed anything else! I wasn't spending more on ads. I didn't add fancy bonuses. I wasn't hustling on sales calls. The *only* thing I did differently was make people laugh with a funny ad. And guess what? It **doubled my traffic** and **doubled my sales** almost instantly.

Imagine creating just ONE silly video and it doubling your sales, not just for a day, but for *weeks* or even *months* at a time! That's exactly what happened. I knew I had stumbled onto something BIG, something I wasn't seeing a lot of people doing online. And I was hooked.

Funny videos became my secret weapon, my golden ticket. And all it took was that one random toilet sitting in my mom's backyard to show me the way. Who knew a broken toilet could lead to freedom? Life is weird like that. But hey, I'm not complaining.

LESSONS LEARNED:

- *Creating Funny Ads is the best way to get an explosion of traffic and attention. ATTENTION is what every business thrives on.*
- *Start With What You Have: Fancy equipment and big budgets are great, but they're not necessary. A few random props, a cell phone, and some creativity are more than enough to make something amazing.*
- *Use Your Resources Creatively: Whether it's a backyard toilet, a rocking horse, or some oranges, you can turn anything into an opportunity if you think outside the box.*
- *Humor Builds Connection: A funny ad doesn't just sell, it creates trust and makes your brand likable. It brings down people's walls and disarms them. In a world where consumers don't trust most companies, making them laugh gives them warm fuzzy feelings inside, and your customers relate those feelings to your products and services!*

THE ART OF BEING RIDICULOUS

I was over the moon. My new book was selling a ton, musicians were seeing amazing results, and my ads were raking in views like nothing I'd ever experienced. Those views turned into a flood of clicks, and those clicks turned into a mountain of sales. It was especially surreal because most of what I was selling were just $19 eBooks that required zero additional effort on my part. Someone would buy a book, get it emailed to them automatically when they purchased, and that was the end of it. Easy peasy.

My nights were still spent taking care of my son and breastfeeding, and I wasn't actively working on my business because, well, taking care of a newborn is a full-time gig. Yet somehow, my business was making more money than I'd ever seen in my life. It gave me security, and I thanked God every day.

The real MVP of this time in my life was my mom. She would come home after long workdays and help with my son, giving me some time to focus on the business. Without her, finishing my books would have taken a lot longer, and she helped me keep what was left of my sanity so that I could pour it into my work.

I'd borrow her car when she got off of work each day and continue to drive into town to upload videos since we still didn't have internet that was strong enough for me to upload videos.

Around this time, I needed knee surgery. Remember that fall I mentioned earlier? I had fallen in a casino when I was pregnant, and it left me with lasting injuries that finally needed to be fixed. My mom watched my son as I flew back to Vegas for X-rays for a few days. While I was there, I had an idea: why not shoot a new ad for my book?

I started to put together some new ideas.

I took stock of what I had at home that I could use in the ad: some bottles of alcohol, my car, my bathroom, a couch, a staircase, a tiny piano, a baby grand piano, and a few family members who were willing to humor me. I also randomly ordered an inflatable lama from Amazon. I felt like I was constantly playing a game show. Like, "Here are ten random props and locations. Now go and make an ad out of it!"

I wrote a script and started filming with my cell phone. I created a concept about a musician completely spiraling because they didn't have enough Spotify followers. I wanted to poke fun at the pressure musicians feel to "make it." I acted like I was losing my mind while crying on a staircase, sitting in my car ranting, and even pretending to be drunk while saying, "What are you talking about? I'm fine!"

There were plenty of over-the-top moments. I punched the inflatable llama in a bathtub, wore a clown wig while pretending my kitchen was on fire, and played the piano like someone who hadn't slept in days. It was ridiculous, but we all had such a blast. I was reminded how much fun creating videos could be. Business can sometimes be boring, but marketing? That should ALWAYS be fun! :)

When I posted the ad, I wasn't prepared for what happened. It took off almost immediately, with people commenting, sharing, and laughing at the absurdity of it all. I had even more views, comments, shares, and SALES than before! I couldn't believe it. What really surprised me was how many people said, "This is so relatable!" "This is me!"

Watch the
"Therapist" ad
by scanning
the QR code.

SCAN ME

You don't need a huge budget or a professional comedy background to make this work. All you need is a willingness to lean into the silliness and not take yourself too seriously. The key is to exaggerate your customer's pain points in a way that makes them laugh and makes them feel understood.

And the best part? Anyone can do this.

In the next chapter, I'll share the 3-step formula I used to create funny ads that worked and how you can use it to transform your business, too. Let's dive in!

3 STEPS TO MAKE FUNNY ADS FOR ANY BUSINESS

L et's get real: *everyone* thinks their business is too boring or serious for funny ads. I hear it all the time: "But my business isn't funny! There's nothing funny about it!"

Unless you're selling whoopie cushions or fart spray, every business is boring. The good news? Funny Ads can be made about any business. They are the best ways to sell your products. Period.

In the beginning of this book I talked about Geico Car Insurance! Is car insurance typically funny? Not exactly laugh-out-loud stuff, right? Yet Geico has built an empire on funny marketing.

We also talked about Dollar Shave Club previously. They sell razors. Exciting? No. Hilarious? Not really. Yet they were able to make fun and entertaining ads that helped them blow up (in a good way) and helped the company sell for a cool **$1 billion in cash.**

And here's a fun fact: it costs $7 million for 30 seconds of Super Bowl ad space. The majority of those ads? Funny. Why? Because the biggest companies in the world have tested all sorts of ads and know that funny ads consistently deliver the best results.

Translation: **funny sells.**

The best part? You don't need millions of dollars to pull it off. With my simple "3-Step Funny Ads Formula," you'll learn how to make even the most "serious" business hilarious and profitable.

My "3-Step Funny Ads Formula"

Ask yourself these three questions in this order.

1. Who is my customer?
2. What are their pain points?
3. How do I exaggerate their pain points?

Step 1: Who Is My Customer?

Before you start brainstorming, figure out who your ideal customer is that you want to target for this ad. Are they moms? Entrepreneurs? Fitness junkies? Be specific! The reason why this is important is because we have to pinpoint exactly what types of things they will relate to. If your ideal customer is a mom, is cracking jokes about football and drinking beer going to be relatable to all of them? No. So we first have to keep in mind what they will relate to and identify with.

Step 2: What Are Their Pain Points?

We've talked about the importance of this before, but let's do it again! Ask yourself, *What's keeping my customers up at night? What are they struggling with? What's that big, annoying problem they desperately want to fix?*

For example:

- Your customer wants to lose weight (pain point).
- They hate exercising (another pain point).
- They hate eating kale and boring foods

Step 3: How Do I Exaggerate Their Pain Points?

Here's the fun part: turn their pain into something they can laugh at. Exaggerate their struggle, make it relatable, and show the ridiculous side of their problem. If you know someone who wants to lose weight but hates eating boring foods like kale, you could show someone sadly eating kale as they're crying and their makeup is falling down their face. Your opening line could be, "Do you want to lose weight but can't stand the thought of having to eat kale ever again?" See how that exaggerates the pain of someone who hates eating kale?

Your goal isn't to make *everyone* laugh. Your aim is to connect with your *ideal customers* and make *them* laugh. Not everyone can relate to someone sadly eating kale, but that's okay. We're not trying to resonate with the whole world. What matters is that your ideal customer feels seen, understands that you can solve their specific problem, and finds humor in the unique challenges they're facing. That's how you create a lasting connection.

For example:

- In the "Toilet" ad, I joked about musicians wasting time doing random things like sitting on the toilet for 25 minutes instead of promoting their music. Musicians loved it because they saw themselves in the ad and knew this was something so many of them were guilty of.
- In the "Therapist" ad, I played a wild, stressed-out artist. I exaggerated feelings of going crazy trying to promote your music and musicians knew the feeling!

The key? Dial up the pain points and make them hilariously absurd but still relatable.

I break down the formula even more in the free training that comes along with this book.

Scan the QR code to watch:

SCAN ME

---

9 TYPES OF FUNNY ADS

I'm about to show you 9 specific types of funny ads that have driven massive sales for my business and the clients that we make funny ads for. Plus, I'll break down how to apply the 3-step formula to each one. These are super simple, and I'll even include video examples so you can easily create them for your business!"

FUNNY AD #1: "WHAT I THOUGHT IT WOULD BE LIKE"

This type of ad shows the difference between how people imagine things will go and how messy they really are!

In the example I am about to share, I used my 3-step formula for an ad I made for my company, where I help entrepreneurs build successful online businesses. I wanted to target moms. Here's what I came up with.

- **Who is my customer?** Moms who want to start or scale their own businesses.
- **What are their pain points?** Trying to juggle being a mom and running a business.
- **How do I exaggerate their pain points?**
  - I pretend to be on a Zoom call while my kid bounces off the walls like he just drank a gallon of soda.
  - I shove a McDonald's Egg McMuffin into my kid's mouth while everything is falling apart around me.
  - I try to stay calm on a sales call while my son is screaming for attention.

This is how the video played out. First, I had a headline over the beginning of the video that read, "What I thought it would look like." It showed me and my son living a stress-free life together and business going great. I have beautiful, peaceful music playing in the background, and the videos of us eating, sleeping, and living life together are in slow motion.

Then, in the next scene, it says, "What it's really like," and that's where the chaos begins. I have frantic music playing, and I play out all the pain points of what "mompreneurs" feel throughout their chaotic day. It was ridiculous, exaggerated, and my son and I had so much fun recording it together. The result? Mompreneurs were saying, "OMG, this is totally me!"

**You can view
this type of ad
by scanning the QR code
on your phone.**

SCAN ME

How can you create this type of ad? Just fill in the blanks below!

- What I thought it was going to be like [customer's pain point].
  - IE: *as a teacher, as a life coach, as a parent, as a fitness coach.*

You can also fill it out alternatively like this:

- "What I thought it was going to be like [insert painful task your customer hates.]
  - IE: *filing my own taxes, investing in real estate without a coach, getting in shape.*

Then after showing visuals of the beautiful experience you "thought it would be like", the next headline would say "What it's really like". This is the fun part where you get to exaggerate how bad it is in a hilarious way!

FUNNY AD #2: "BEGINNER VS. EXPERT" AD

As I mentioned earlier, in one of my businesses, *Laugh My Ads Off,* I help entrepreneurs learn how to build successful online businesses. In a previous ad, I focused on targeting moms who struggle to grow their business while juggling the demands of motherhood. This time, I decided to tackle a different challenge. This is one that many entrepreneurs of all genders face:

Here's how I used my "3-Step Funny Ads Formula" to address this pain point:

- **Who is my customer?** Digital entrepreneurs
- **What are their pain points?** Getting anxiety when it's time to do their pitch and also raising their prices.
- **How do I exaggerate their pain points?** Show myself through various scenarios completely unable to say my prices. My mouth won't form the words, I say the wrong prices, and I freeze.

Once the "3-Step Funny Ads Formula" is followed, now we can decide how we want to entertain our audience.

I decided to entertain the viewer by creating a **Beginner vs. Expert** ad. It was super simple and crazy effective and involved two characters.

- **The Beginner:** This is your customer (played by you but in a costume, wig, mustache, etc.), the person struggling with all the problems your audience faces. In this case, they're terrified of pitching prices or asking for what they're worth.
- **The Expert:** This is YOU playing yourself "the expert". You swoop in like a hero with all the answers, showing them how to solve their problem and boost their confidence.

Here's the magic: **You play both roles!** By switching between characters, you keep the ad entertaining and relatable.

You can also add a call to action at the very end. For example, if you're a coach, the Beginner could say, "How can I stop feeling so awkward about my prices?"

And the Expert could reply, "Click the link to grab my free PDF!" (I don't always pitch in my videos. Sometimes I pitch my offer in the description)

Check out the "Slap-Raising Prices" video.

Scan the QR code:

SCAN ME

If you're nervous about trying something like this, remember: **humor doesn't have to be perfect. It just has to be real.** Your audience will appreciate your effort to make them smile while solving their problems. So give it a try!

FUNNY AD #3: MAKING SERIOUS TOPICS FUNNY WITHOUT BEING MEAN

What if you're a coach for people dealing with real trauma? Is it even okay to be funny when you're working with heavy, emotional stuff? Actually, YES! It's not only okay, it's a golden opportunity. Humor can help people in pain feel just a little better. There are a couple of rules I follow if I don't want to offend people.

For example: If you're helping someone who's lost a loved one, you can't just be like, "Hey, remember when your mom died? Good times, right?" (Every time I say this on stage, people laugh, and I have to let them know they're all going to hell.)

So, how *do* you add humor to something serious?

The Golden Rule is to Not Hurt Anyone's Feelings: Don't Make Fun of People's Pain

Here's a way to think about it: If your friend runs into a pole, you don't laugh *at* them, at least, not right away. (Although, full disclosure, when my friend ran into a pole at an indoor playground last week chasing my son, their face was bleeding, and my first reaction was to laugh. I know, I'm a terrible person. I've already accepted it.) But for most *normal* people, you'd probably wait until you're sure they're okay, and then laugh about it *together* later!

Here's what you CAN make fun of that doesn't hurt anyone's feelings:

- The silly things your customer does which lead to their big problem.
- The weird ways they try to fix things.

One of my favorite examples is a skit that hilariously pokes fun at ignoring glaring red flags in relationships.

Scene 1: (Read this in an obnoxious California girl accent)

Girl 1: "The other day, I tried to check my boyfriend's phone, and he snatched it away from me!"

Girl 2: "Wow, that means he really respects his privacy!"

Girl 1: "Exactly! That's what I'm *sayinggggggg!*"

The title of the video is "How Women Ignore Red Flags." There's another scene that goes something like this:

Girl 1: "*Guuuurl*, He doesn't pay for anything!"

Girl 2: "Wow, that means he's not materialistic."

Girl 1: "I know!! Isn't it amazing?????!!"

Watch "How Women Ignore Red Flags" by scanning the QR code.

It's definitely worth it.

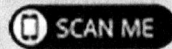

SCAN ME

See what the girl's conversation is doing there? They're not making fun of someone being in a bad or abusive relationship. They're poking fun at how we sometimes ignore obvious warning signs that get us to that thing that causes the pain.

If the creator were a trauma coach or therapist, they could've ended that video with:

"Ready to heal from that narcissistic relationship you were in? Download my free guide at [website]."

Now, THAT'S a funny, relatable ad that sells a solution without crossing any lines.

I like to say that I've learned how to turn pain into profit.
Something that would normally hurt can actually do the opposite.
It can make you laugh, AND make you a whole lot of money.
This is how you win at life.

LESSONS LEARNED:

- **Pick the Right Target**
  - *Never laugh AT the person's traumatic incident.*
  - *DO laugh at the silly things we do that get us in our mess!*
  - *Make fun of red flags, not the people who missed them.*
- **End with Hope**
  - *Always wrap up with a solution (your products/services, of course!)*
  - *Give them something actionable to do next.*
- **Stay in the Safe Zone**
  - *If you're wondering, "Is this too far?" it probably is.*
  - *Remember: we're healing with humor, not hurting with it.*

The Big Secret: If you can make someone laugh about their struggles while showing them a way forward, you've not just made a sale - you've made a difference!

FUNNY AD #4: "BEFORE AND AFTER AD"

TAMALES & PANTY DROPPERS: I START AN ADS AGENCY

One day, while scrolling through Facebook, I saw a familiar face pop up in my feed: my friend Billy. Billy owns a cologne company, and being the curious person I am, I reached out.

"How's it going?" I asked.

"We're getting sales," he said, "but it's not profitable."

I dug a little deeper and discovered two things: he was running ads to a Shopify-style store instead of a funnel, and more importantly, the name of his cologne was *Liquid Panty Remover*.

Yes, you read that correctly. *Liquid. Panty. Remover.*

I couldn't stop laughing. Offensive? Maybe. Hilarious and dripping with opportunity for funny ads? Absolutely.

I made him an offer: "I'll build you a funnel, create funny ads, and let's split the profits 50/50." He agreed, and just like that, I was officially in the cologne business.

But the real question loomed: *How do you make cologne funny?*

Usually, I start by exaggerating a pain point. But for Liquid Panty Remover, I flipped the script. I created a new 3-step formula for a new type of humor where you exaggerate the result someone wants, instead of the pain point they currently have.

1. **Who is my customer?**
   - Men who want to be more attractive and confident.
2. **What results do they want? (Instead of what pain points do they have)**
   - To feel irresistible to women and have women notice them.
3. **How do I exaggerate those results?**
   - Show that this cologne is so powerful, it makes women fall all over the user instantly, to the point of absurdity.

Back in New Mexico, where Wi-Fi was still practically nonexistent, I got to work. I started brainstorming ideas that would exaggerate the results. What's the most outrageous benefit a guy could get from wearing cologne?

I thought it would be funny to show that before using the cologne, a lonely guy is invisible to women. He's scared about his future. After using it? Instant rockstar status. Women everywhere would be practically throwing themselves at him.

Great idea, right? There was just one problem: COVID. I couldn't get anybody together because nobody was leaving their house.

I did what any reasonable person would do in this situation: I went to Walmart and bought dolls. One male doll, two Barbies, and suddenly, I had my cast.

So there I was, holding dolls, doing different voices like a five-year-old playing make-believe:

The script basically went like this:

Male doll: Oh no, I'm so lonely. Women don't want me, and I'm going to die alone.

Me: (Sprays cologne on him)

Female doll 1: Oh Billy! I love you.

Female doll 2: I love you too, Billy. Mwah, Mwah, Mwah! (Proceeds to kiss Billy 5 times.)

Male doll: Oh no, what am I gonna do? All these women want me. How am I going to choose just one?

Female doll 2: Don't worry Billy, you don't have to choose one of us. You can have us both.

Was it ridiculous? Yes. Did people love it? Surprisingly, no one found it offensive that I was talking about having a polyamorous relationship using children's Barbie dolls.

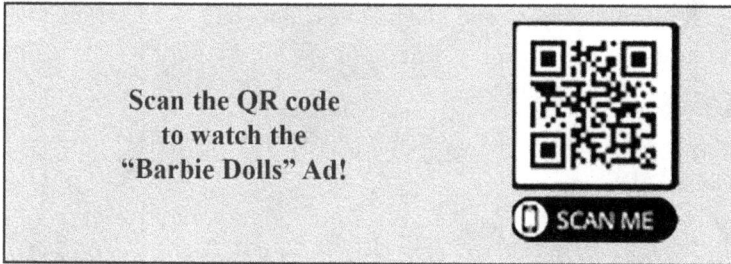

Scan the QR code
to watch the
"Barbie Dolls" Ad!

SCAN ME

From this ad, I learned a brand new way to make things entertaining. In the previous chapters, I talked about exaggerating the *pain points* of your customers. With this new strategy, you would exaggerate the *results* that your customers could get when they use your products or services. These are two simple formulas *you* can now follow too!

Within weeks, we were making thousands a day in sales. The demand was insane. So insane that we ran out of cologne.

Then we got the bad news. The cologne came from France, and COVID had turned the shipping industry into a hot mess. Boats were delayed for months. Even when they made it to the U.S., shipments got stuck at ports.

We had no choice but to stop scaling our ads. We had no product to ship. I updated the funnel to say: *"Due to COVID: This cologne is on back-order and will be shipped once the new shipments arrive."*

Even when COVID disrupted the supply chain and we ran out of cologne, people *still* placed orders. That's the power of funny ads. They apparently create demand even for cologne people can't smell and won't receive for months.

After seeing the success of Liquid Panty Remover, I realized something important: this formula works for anything.

For example, I tested it out with my dad's tamale business. I used the same steps to create a funny ad and shot it right in the same backyard I'd been using for all my other ads. And guess what? Sales took off! (Turns out, my parents' backyard had officially become a full-blown Hollywood studio.)

In just a few months, I was running funny ads and funnels for cologne, tamales, and my info product business teaching musicians. I was officially an "agency." I was creating funnels and funny ads for multiple niches and companies and all were profitable. AMAZING!

LESSONS LEARNED: HOW TO SELL ANYTHING WITH FUNNY ADS

- *We have covered two simple ways to make ANY ad Funny:*
  - *Exaggerate the pain points (like we covered in previous chapters).*
  - *Exaggerate the results your customers want to hilarious levels (like making cologne seem like a magic love potion).*
- *Opportunity is Everywhere:*
  - *You don't need your own product.*
  - *You can partner with existing businesses by either charging a flat fee, participating in profit sharing, or do both like I do.*
- *Funny Ads Work for EVERYTHING:*
  - *If you can sell cologne with Barbies...*
  - *And tamales from a backyard...*
  - *You can sell literally anything.*

And last, If you don't have friends or actors, just use dolls!!

MY FACE ALMOST DETACHES FROM
MY SKULL

I shared how I used exaggeration to make the cologne ad with the Barbies in the previous chapter, but I wanted to share a couple more examples that will hopefully spark some ideas in your own head!

The more exaggerated and comical the benefits, the more memorable (and shareable) your ad will be.

Chevrolet created an ad that I LOVE. This one is great because they exaggerate the feeling that the young man has when he thinks he is getting the car of his dreams. He is singing, dancing, and as the ad progresses, it gets funnier and funnier.

**Check out the
Chevrolet ad
by scanning
the QR code.**

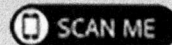

SCAN ME

For an ad we created with life coach Brooke Castillo, we decided to take exaggeration to another level, so far, in fact, that the "after" result ended up being something nobody would ever want. So why would we do that? I'll explain.

Brooke was promoting her upcoming live conference, and we wanted the ad to showcase the transformation people could experience by attending, But just like the previous chapters have mentioned, we decided to use exaggeration to add humor.

Here's how we used my 3-step formula.

Step 1: Who is my customer?

Our audience was people who felt stuck and unmotivated in their lives.

Step 2: What results do they want?

They wanted to feel confident, alive, and like the best version of themselves.

Step 3: How do I exaggerate those results?

We would exaggerate how amazing and beautiful a person could feel after attending this event but go so far that it would be ridiculous.

Here's how it ended up going! We started the ad with me in pajamas, slouched over on a couch, looking like someone who'd completely lost their motivation to live. I had messy hair, zero energy, and gave off a hopeless vibe.

Brooke appeared, talking about how the audience should join her life-changing event! That's when the transformation scene came in. Brooke said, "You're going to become so confident, you're not even going to know what to do with your sexy self!"

At this point, I magically changed into a sleek dress, standing tall and exuding confidence, or so that was the plan. You know those dramatic beauty commercials where a woman's hair blows in slow motion, looking effortlessly glamorous and untouchable? Yeah, we *didn't* do that. Instead of a professional wind machine, we used a mega-powerful weed blower. We blasted it in my face. My hair went in every direction, and my skin flapped so hard it looked like my face was trying to detach from my skull. It wasn't exactly "glamorous," but it was entertaining to watch and we laughed so hard we cried.

Sure, nobody actually *wants* their face blown halfway off by a weed blower, but they do want to feel confident. And we exaggerated how someone would feel if wind was in their face in slow motion. The message was clear. Join the event to get your confidence back, but we used fun visuals and exaggeration to grab their attention.

> **Scan the QR code to watch the ad we did with Brooke Castillo.**
>
> SCAN ME

The biggest takeaway? Exaggeration is comedy gold in ads! Blow those pain points out of proportion or hype up the results your customers want. It'll get laughs and, more importantly, it'll make people excited to buy!

IMPORTANT NOTE: Please don't try stuff if you're not sure it's safe. The last thing I need is an email saying, *"Well, you said you put a weed blower in your face without knowing if your head would explode, so I decided to put my phone in the toaster for my video and see if it would charge."* Yeah... let's not do that.

FUNNY AD #5: "ANTI-TESTIMONIAL AD"

HOW TO SELL A TON OF YOUR STUFF BY TELLING PEOPLE NOT TO BUY YOUR STUFF

I had the pleasure of creating a fun ad for Russell Brunson's business conference, "Funnel Hacking Live." He had also invited me to speak at the event, so I was excited to join the lineup and wanted to create something unforgettable. I was very honored especially, since Russell's books were what played such a huge role in me earning my first few million dollars and now I get to speak at his conference? Dream. Come. True.

Previously, During my "Make Funny Ads and Videos" challenge, one of my attendees, Tom Camp, sent me a hilarious testimonial video he made for me. In it, he told everyone *not* to join my challenge, but in a creative way. For example, he joked that if you joined, you'd make so much money that you'd have to deal with "scumbags" like lawyers and bankers.

And so, the "Anti-Testimonial Ad" was born! This is where you *complain* about having the things people usually dream of having. It's like flipping the script, and it works like magic.

For the ad for Funnel Hacking Live, I decided to talk about all the horrible ways my life changed since working with Russell Bruson and attending the conference myself.

I complained about having "too much time to spend with my son playing video games" now that my business was automated. I complained about my phone going off all the time with "purchase notifications" and showed a clip of me in bed being awoken by obnoxious "you just got paid" texts dinging all night. I couldn't stop ranting about how I kept getting sunburned from working on my laptop outside since I had the ability to work from anywhere. The complaints went on and on.

Keep in mind that most of my ads were created with me and my sibling "True." The same sibling that I made funny videos with since we were kids. We're still doing the same thing!

We sent the finished video to their media team. After running the ad for weeks, their ads buyer sent me the numbers, and we were excited to learn that our ad brought in 2X the amount of traffic and 6X their engagement average. I watched as hundreds of comments flooded in!

In my entire life of creating ads, I had never seen so many compliments. It feels so good to pour your heart into something and then seeing people enjoy it. Making money is fun, but I'd say knowing that something you created is liked and appreciated by people might feel even better. I knew this type of ad was a winner!

Scan the QR code to check out the "Anti-Testimonial Ad" we created for Russell Brunson's Funnel Hacking Live event.

SCAN ME

Here are some of the comments that came in for Russell Brunson's event!

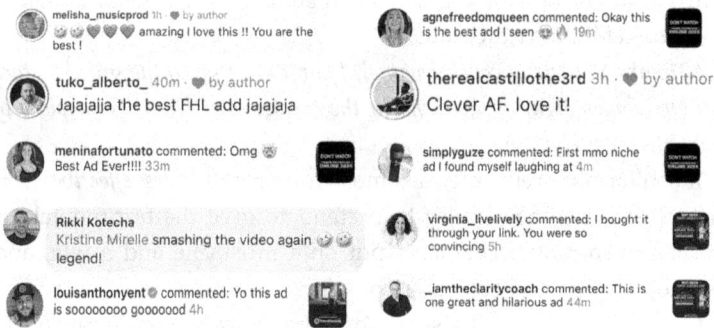

melisha_musicprod 1h · 💙 by author
😍 😍 💚 💚 💚 amazing I love this !! You are the best !

agnefreedomqueen commented: Okay this is the best add I seen 👏 🔥 19m

tuko_alberto_ 40m · 💙 by author
Jajajajja the best FHL add jajajaja

therealcastillothe3rd 3h · 💙 by author
Clever AF. love it!

meninafortunato commented: Omg 😂 Best Ad Ever!!!! 33m

simplyguze commented: First mmo niche ad I found myself laughing at 4m

Rikki Kotecha
Kristine Mirelle smashing the video again 😂 😂 legend!

virginia_livelively commented: I bought it through your link. You were so convincing 5h

louisanthonyent 🔵 commented: Yo this ad is sooooooooo gooooood 4h

_iamtheclaritycoach commented: This is one great and hilarious ad 44m

So how can you create an anti-testimonial ad?

Here's how to do it using my 3-step formula:

USING MY 3-STEP FORMULA FOR THE ANTI-TESTIMONIAL AD

Step 1: Who is my customer?

Entrepreneurs and business owners who want to grow their businesses and learn from the best in the industry.

Step 2: What results do they want?

To grow their revenue, have more time with family, connect with other like-minded individuals, provide for their children, and make lots of money.

Step 3: How do I exaggerate those results?

Complain about actually achieving all of the entrepreneurs' goals, but making it seem like it ruined their life.

Want another example? Imagine you're a dating coach. The "customer" doing the testimonial could complain that ever since they took your dating course, they can't even leave the house anymore because women throw themselves at them everywhere. The scenes could show them at the grocery store grabbing milk and women holding onto their ankles. There could be a scene with a guy trying to drive down the street and women sliding down the windshield trying to get in. It's ridiculous.

"Thanks to [dating coach's name], I can't even go to the grocery store without women fighting over me in the bread aisle! I feel like a piece of meat. My life is chaos now!"

It's hilarious, relatable, an, most importantly, it's *effective*. You can either get someone else to pretend to give the testimonial, or you can even play a character, put on a mustache and a wig, and pretend to be a "mad customer" of yours.

Go ahead and give it a shot! You'll be amazed at how much fun (and how many sales) you'll have.

FUNNY AD #6: "HORROR MOVIES AND SPANISH TALK SHOWS"
HOW TO CREATE SPOOFS AND PARODIES

A spoof or parody is when you take something everyone knows, like a movie or commercial, and give it your own hilarious twist. It's like telling an inside joke that everyone gets.

One of the first spoofs we ever created was an ad that looked like a typical *scary movie trailer*. You know the ones: some creepy monster lurking in the shadows, a girl running for her life (but still looking flawless), and that intense music that screams *something terrible is about to happen!*

I made up two characters: The "Spotify Demon," a masked, creepy monster who haunts musicians when their music isn't heard, and a fortune teller who warns me of my doom unless I get my music out there. Naturally, the only way to stop this madness is by getting my book.

Scan the QR code to check out the "Spotify Demon" scary movie spoof.

SCAN ME

This was my first ad shot with a professional camera. I invested in equipment during this time to upgrade the production. We used random props, like an old guitar and a creepy mask I found online, and I dragged a few friends to help me out. We added some dramatic music and quick cuts, and boom! A scary movie spoof was born.

A few years later, I was working with Brooke Castillo to promote her latest book for life coaches. She wanted something fun and creative to promote the release, so I decided to create a spoof of a Spanish Talk Show. They're a little over the top and dramatic. I created a character named "Maria," who was the over-the-top host of a Spanish talk show. Brooke came on as my "special guest," and together, we talked about her book, *How to Do It*, a guide for aspiring life coaches to launch their own coaching businesses.

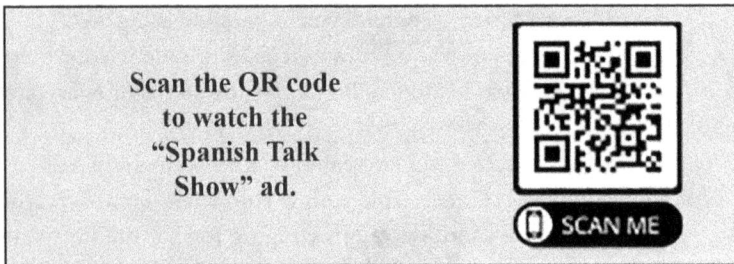

> **Scan the QR code to watch the "Spanish Talk Show" ad.**
>
> SCAN ME

If you notice, Maria is playing the role of one of Brooke's skeptical customers, asking questions like, "But how much does it cost? What if we don't believe we can actually become life coaches?" Brooke responds to every objection and shows that her book is the ultimate solution.

That's the magic of these ads. They all deliver the same core message but in fun, creative, and engaging ways. We're always showing potential customers that we understand their struggles and have the perfect solution to help them overcome them.

HOW TO WRITE YOUR OWN SPOOF

C reating a spoof is one of the most creative and entertaining types of videos you can make, and they're ridiculously fun to create.

But how do you come up with ideas for spoofs, especially if you don't consider yourself super creative?

Step 1: Find Inspiration in What's Popular

Start by making a list of things you've seen in popular culture, media, or ads.

Here are some examples to spark your brainstorming:

- Motivational movie scenes
- Reality TV shows
- Dating shows
- News broadcasts
- Home improvement shows
- Talent contest shows
- A specific scene in a movie
- Prescription commercials
- Action movies

From there, look for subcategories or iconic moments. For example, in the *Action Movie* category, you might remember the famous *Terminator* line: "Come with me if you want to live." If you're a fitness instructor, you could spoof that by saying, "Come with me if you want to get in shape!" It's fun, recognizable, and connects to your message. (PS. You don't have to go that cheesy. I just enjoy the ridiculousness)

Step 2: Pick a Concept That Fits Your Brand

Think about how your product or service can fit into a spoof. Make sure your ideal customer will recognize what you are making fun of. For example, if your audience is women, doing a spoof on WWE wrestling isn't going to resonate. But doing a spoof on a dating show might crush!

Step 3: Get Creative With What You Have

Spoofs and Parodies don't require a massive budget. Just get creative with your surroundings and resources. For Russell Brunson's *Selling Online* event, we created a parody of the song "12 Days of Christmas." It was fun because the event was right before Christmas.

To make it happen, I used a local furniture shop for the shoot, rounded up a few friends to play actors, and even held auditions at a local acting school. Acting schools are great for finding affordable, eager talent. Aspiring actors are often excited to be part of fun projects, especially if it helps build their portfolio, so they're typically fun to work with!

Check out our finished "12 Days of Christmas" ad.

Scan the QR code:

SCAN ME

Step 4: Plan Your Shoot

Once you've nailed down your concept, location, and actors, start planning the shoot. Here are a few things to keep in mind:

- **Write a Simple Script**: Don't overcomplicate it. With these types of ads, it's easy to go "too far." This means that you could easily go off track. You may create tons of dialogue that is fun and entertaining, but doesn't stick to talking about the pain points your products solve. Remember, it's all about the customer, and all they care about is what's in it for them.
- **Scout Locations**: Use what's available, your house, a park, or even a friend's business.

There are also websites that have prebuilt creative spaces that you can rent by the hour. Do a quick internet search for "local photography studios" or "local video studios" and see what comes up!

- **Gather Props and Costumes and Rehearse and Improvise!**

Shoots never go exactly as planned, so always have a good attitude, be prepared to pivot when necessary, and rule #1, always have fun.

Growing up, I loved courtroom dramas like "Judge Judy". So when I needed to create an ad for my business where I teach entrepreneurs how to make funny ads, I thought, why not spoof a courtroom scene? I decided I wanted to play all the characters. I would be the judge, the defendant, and the lawyer. Super fun!

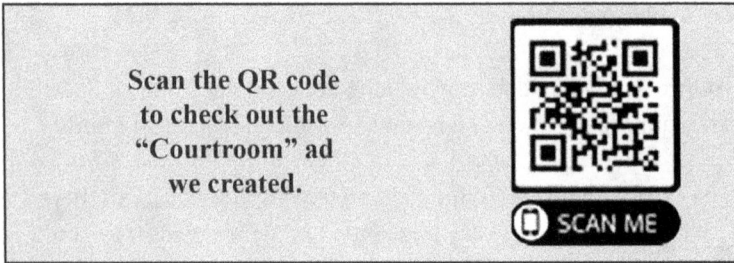

This is another great solution if you don't have actors. You can just play them all yourself! Get a mustache, a wig, use an accent! Your viewers will love you for it!

One of the biggest lessons I've learned from creating ads like this is that they don't even have to be *hilarious* to work. They just need to grab attention. Growing up in New Mexico, I remember seeing these wild ads from this local injury attorney. I remember this one where he dressed up as a chicken, clucking around and saying, "*Bock, bock!* Call me if you've been in an accident!" It didn't necessarily make you laugh out loud, but it entertained you! And it left a lasting impression. His goal wasn't to create a masterpiece, it was to make people remember him when they were injured, and it paid off big time.

LESSONS LEARNED:

- *You can rent creative locations to film your ads. Do an internet search to find available spaces that you could rent by the hour!*
- *You can get actors from a local acting school. Contact the school, send them a proposal with your script, whether there is pay involved, and ask if you can hold an audition there! They're always looking for opportunities to give to their students, so it's a win-win situation.*

FUNNY AD #7: PUSHING BOUNDARIES
SEX AND THE F WORD

To me, the funniest videos are ones that push the lines to the point where large groups of people are offended. Unfortunately, that's not typically good for business. But for fun, you can still create ads that push the lines just barely enough to get people to do a double-take.

I'm going to share a fun and safe way to do that for your audience. This example is where you make them THINK that you are about to say or do something that would normally need to be censored, but then you take it in a different direction. I'll explain:

When I was a kid, there was this rhyme that I liked:

"Miss Suzy had a steamboat, the steamboat had a bell.

Miss Suzy went to heaven, the steamboat went to…

hellll-o operator, please give me number nine…"

The entire rhyme was designed to make you think it was going toward cursing, but only to twist into something harmless. It was clever and funny, and I thought, why not use that concept in an ad?

I started by listing what I had at my disposal:

- A cornfield in front of my house.
- My brother, who is an Army lieutenant, and his team.
- A yoga outfit.
- A green screen and crazy wigs.

- A swimming pool (I would be in Vegas a few weeks later for this final shot).

Using these random elements, I created a script and filmed an ad that played with the idea of pretending we are about to curse, but instead, we segway into a similar-sounding word. This was shot entirely on a cell phone.

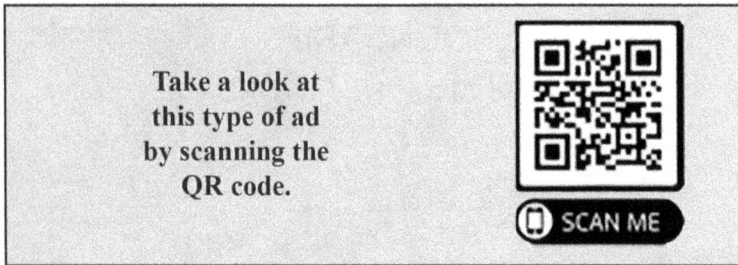

Take a look at
this type of ad
by scanning the
QR code.

SCAN ME

You could do this for your own business using this same concept!

For example, let's say you were a local business that sold fudge! In one scene, you could show someone screaming…

"What the fu…"

[And then cut to a shot of you holding fudge inside your store]

You could then exclaim, "Fuuuuu…dge is the best Christmas gift! Come by our store for homemade walnut fudge!"

Another ad I created was a bit more suggestive.

In the ad, I ask a young man, "How big is it?"

As I glance down below his waist, he says, "It's probably the biggest that you've ever seen in your life."

Then I reply, "But it's not really about how big it is. It's about how you use it."

He asks me if I want to see it, and after showing me whatever "it" is, I say, "Wow, that's huge."

The camera pans out, and it turns out he's holding a massive list of resources for musicians. We continue to talk about why this book is so awesome and then give a call to action at the end so that musicians can buy the list for themselves.

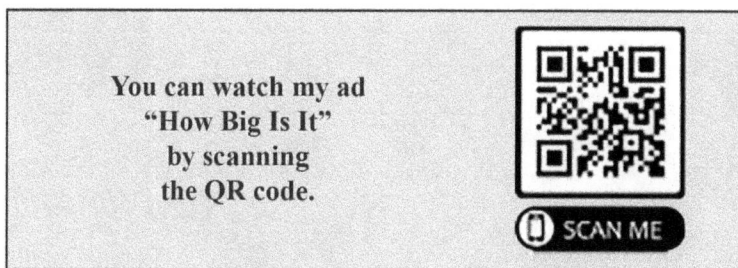

You could use this in *your* business in a variety of ways. Here are a few examples.

A business coach could use it to talk about email lists. The dialogue could open like this...

"How big is it? [looks down below the waist of man] Oh my, it's so tiny!! Why do you have such a small... email list?!"

The camera zooms out to reveal an entrepreneur looking at his lap where there is a computer revealing his small email list. Throw in some more dialogue about what your offer is, how you can help them solve their problem, and then always end with a call to action like *"Sign up for our free training to learn how to build a massive email list in 3 steps!"*

Another example could be a wealth coach making decisions about bank accounts.

"Why is yours so small? What am I supposed to do with this?"

The camera zooms out to show a bank balance of $42 and then the wealth coach transitions to explaining the importance of financial planning.

It doesn't matter what you're selling. Creativity is the secret sauce that makes it work.

CONFESSIONS OF A LINGERIE MODEL

When I was about 23, I was drowning in debt, had no income, and was still clueless about how to make it as a musician. This was before I had my son or ever made a dime from music. Desperate for cash, I signed with a modeling agency and found myself modeling in lingerie at Tao Nightclub on the Las Vegas Strip. For the amazing payment of $125 a night (I hope you can sense my sarcasm), my job was either massaging another girl in lingerie or standing in a cage fanning myself with an oversized fan as people stared at me and took photos, totally normal Tuesday night stuff.

People would walk in and see me and a bunch of other half-naked women on display. Some of the girls were chilling in a bath of water with rose petals strategically placed to cover lady parts. My personal favorite was lying on a bed doing nothing while people stared and took pictures. I had to try everything just to stay awake. :/

One night, I nearly dozed off while lying there in my glamorous display of underwear my broke self had bought from Walmart. They didn't pay enough for me to get the good stuff. As I stared at the ceiling, I kept thinking about how I'd spent years training as a classical pianist and singer. I couldn't help but wonder, *How did I end up here?* No judgment on how anyone earns a living, but this wasn't exactly the career path I had in mind.

That gig as a lingerie model in that nightclub served almost like a "gateway drug" into a dark spiral of bad decisions I made simply because I needed money.

I mentioned in a previous chapter that I had my promising "phone sex operator" job, but it got a little more interesting than that during that time.

One day, I was skimming the internet and saw a Craigslist ad for something called "webcam models." I had never heard the term before, but the ad said you could work from your laptop in a safe environment. I had always dreamed of working from my laptop, so that was my main goal at the time.

I answered the ad, and the guy on the phone explained what a webcam model does. Apparently, most girls log on, strip, or do whatever the guys want, and they get paid by the minute. I needed money so badly that I didn't even stop to think about it. I logged on my first day and just chatted with people, no stripping, no weird stuff, and somehow made a couple hundred bucks. At the time, that felt like winning the lottery.

The next day, I logged on again, but I just wasn't feeling it. It turns out that sitting around and chatting online for cash wasn't exactly my dream job, shocking! I know. And considering I wasn't using any of my actual talents, you can imagine how much I felt like I was totally winning at life.

One day, for no apparent reason, I started being really mean to everyone in my chat rooms. Imagine me telling all these poor guys how worthless they were. But something weird happened, they started paying me more. People actually logged on just to watch me verbally abuse everyone. One day, I even threw on a wig and did the whole thing in a terrible British accent, and somehow, that worked too. People were paying me by the minute to insult them. I saw a lot of comments in the chat room talking about how entertaining and fun it was. I was confused, but I didn't care. Being poor sucked, and I just wanted to not be poor anymore.

My chat rooms started filling up. I called everybody losers and told them how disappointed their moms must be in them, and they just kept coming back. I'll spare all the ridiculous details, but let's just say it was interesting.

I was officially an online dominatrix. I had created this character, and everyone loved her even though she was mean. I was earning from my laptop by verbally abusing men. I realized when I asked the universe for a job where I could work from my laptop, I should have been a little bit more specific.

Not long after this *incredibly promising* career move (yes, sarcasm again), I had enough. This was the time when I decided to head to Hollywood to chase my dream of becoming a singer. I mentioned this in a previous chapter, but I went on Craigslist.com and I found the perfect living arrangement: a kitchen for rent in someone's house. (Because who doesn't dream of living in a kitchen? Fun fact: I've now lived in both a kitchen *and* a garage. How many people can put that on their resumé?)

My kitchen had this little divider, so I had a small amount of privacy. I slept on this military-like cot and had these huge plastic bins from Walmart for my clothes and shoes. The floor was cold tile, and there was this loud, screaming parrot that would never stop yelling.

During this time, the owner of the webcam company offered me a job training other girls because, apparently, I was excelling in this glamorous career path. I could already see my future as a webcam model mogul. Every day, I convinced myself it was fine to push the line a little further. Just a little more each day, no big deal. But I knew deep down it was a terrible idea.

So, instead of accepting the promotion, I just quit. Probably wasn't the answer he was expecting. One evening, I logged in, doing the usual, verbally abusing strangers amongst other nonsense (as one does on a casual afternoon) when Jessie J's song "Who You Are" started playing.

It's a beautiful song, and the lyrics say:

Don't lose who you are
In the blur of the stars
Seeing is deceiving
Dreaming is believing
It's okay not to be okay.

Sometimes it's hard
To follow your heart
Tears don't mean you're losing
Everybody's bruising
Just be true to who you are.

I shut my computer that day. I logged off and was officially *done*. I felt like I was losing myself. I prayed and asked God to help me. I knew I had talent, but I had no idea how to earn from it. I was tired of being broke and doing things I hated for money.

I got a gym membership just so I'd have a place to shower, and I started hunting for spots where I could park my car at night where I was planning to sleep. With no income and no more webcam job, I couldn't afford to keep renting my glamorous Craigslist kitchen.

But within a week, I somehow landed my first gig performing at that hotel in Hollywood. That saved me, and I was able to keep paying rent for my tiny kitchen apartment in North Hollywood.

It reminded me that when you make a decision and walk in faith, things work out. When failure isn't an option, you find a way to succeed.

So why did I tell this long story?

The dominatrix character I created, who degraded men in chat rooms, stayed in my mind for over a decade.

The inspiration for your ads and videos can come from so many things in your life. Have you ever heard the saying "art imitating life"? The art that you create comes from what you experience or observe in your life. Everywhere you turn, there is inspiration for content. You just have to look for it and find the humor in it.

Little did I know, I'd eventually bring that dominatrix character back, this time in front of thousands of people on a massive stage.

FUNNY AD #8: I BECOME THE "ADS DOMINATRIX"

In 2022, when Russell Brunson asked me to speak at Funnel Hacking Live for the first time in front of his live audience of 6,000 people, I was stoked. It's a big deal for entrepreneurs and it felt like the Grammys of the business entrepreneurial world. It was especially a big deal for me since I was so new to online marketing. I really wanted to entertain the massive audience of people who came from all around the world to be there. As I mentioned before, Russell's teachings were life-changing for me, so it was magical to share his stage.

I had been to my first Funnel Hacking Live event one year before and had the life-changing experience of walking across the stage to accept an award for earning my first million dollars. It had only been a short time period after releasing my ad that I made with a toilet and a cell phone.

Now I get to speak at that same conference? Let's *gooooo!*

I was excited to share my story about using funny ads to make millions and show the audience how they could do it too. I also wanted to introduce my funny ads agency, where we create hilarious, attention-grabbing ads for businesses. My goal was to inspire new entrepreneurs to grow their businesses with fun video content while also attracting clients who wanted us to bring their marketing to life with a touch of humor.

But simply saying, "Hey, I make video ads for businesses,"

sounded boring. So, I decided to spice things up. That's when I brought "Ads Dominatrix" to life.

I found an office to film in and asked a few guys working there if they wanted to be in the ad. They agreed, and I got into my costume, a leather outfit I surprisingly found on Amazon. I had a leather stick, started yelling at the guys about their terrible marketing, and just went for it.

I don't always use a script. I like to wing it with an outline and see what happens. Apparently, that was a lot for the two volunteers. After a few takes, they bailed. I wasn't sure if they were confused, offended, or just plain weirded out. Either way, I kept going because, hey, the show must go on.

Surprisingly, they came back a little later with a change of heart. I guess it's not every day you get the chance to be in a bizarre commercial where a woman in a ridiculous costume critiques your marketing choices by beating you up. By the end, everyone was laughing and having a blast.

One of the guys even got so into it that he volunteered to bend over and take his pants off for the scene. (Don't worry. It's not as bad as it sounds. Or maybe it is?)

On the morning of my Funnel Hacking Live presentation, I was pumped to show the ad during my presentation. But a few hours before the big moment, the events' lawyers watched it and immediately gave it the axe. Apparently, "family-friendly" doesn't include dominatrix humor.

I did try to argue my case, though. After all, the speaker before me gave a whole presentation loudly discussing vaginas and having sex with his wife, but hey, who's comparing? My ad was basically *Sesame Street* following him. Still, I respected their decision and played a censored version. I still had a blast even though I had to put "censored" text over like half of the ad.

> **To check out the uncensored version of my "Ads Dominatrix" ad**
>
> SCAN ME

I've spoken at a lot of events since then, but that one was the most unforgettable for me. Up until that point, I didn't really think I had much to offer the entrepreneurial world. Honestly, I kind of figured everyone already knew how to make content.

Turns out, what feels easy to you might be someone else's biggest challenge. Never underestimate the power of what you know and how it can change the lives of others.

After my talk, people came up to me saying they finally felt "free" and didn't care what anyone thought about them on camera anymore. One person even ran to the bathroom, started brushing their teeth on a video, talked about their products, and told me it got the most engagement they'd ever had.

It was really fun seeing the impact it had. They weren't just learning. They were taking action. It was amazing to see, and it felt good to play a small part in their entrepreneurial journey.

For you, there's probably something that comes naturally, something you don't think twice about either, but others find difficult. Share it with the world! You might be surprised at the difference you can make. Not only will it remind you that you're on the right path, but it could also lead to a product, service, course, or idea that makes more money than you ever imagined.

HOW TO CREATE CHARACTERS

C reating characters for funny ads is like playing dress-up for a purpose, and it's my absolute favorite part of the job! One of the best examples of a company nailing this is Geico's caveman ads. If you remember those, in one ad, there's a TV anchor that says, "Geico. It's so easy even a caveman can do it!" And then, *bam!* Camera zooms out, and a caveman is standing there the whole time, overhears him, and storms out offended. It's hilarious because it's so unexpected. That campaign became super popular, and it shows how a great character can make your message stick.

When I start to create characters, there are a few things I do first:

I visit Amazon.com for ideas or Halloween Costume stores for ideas! I once stumbled across an elderly woman's costume on Amazon. Naturally, I started thinking, *How can I possibly tie this character into selling my book to musicians?*

I created a "3-Step Funny Ads Formula," but for creating characters: Here's how it goes.

- **Who is my Customer?** Musicians
- **What is their pain point:** Growing old and being afraid people won't hear their music
- **How can I exaggerate it by using a character?** Dress up as an elderly woman and then also show the exaggerated

version of a man who waited too long to follow his dreams, and now he's dead. (It's a lot less worse than it sounds)

I created two different characters, shot it on a cell phone, and all in just a few minutes. Super simple! Believe it or not, this ad did fantastic and brought in a ton of sales for my book.

To check my simple "Grandma" ad that we shot in just a few minutes, **Scan the QR code:**	SCAN ME

In this next ad, I also played a grandma, but unlike the previous ad that took minutes to shoot, we spent about half a day shooting this one. We have different scenes, characters, props, and more. This is an example of a higher-budget video where I rented a location and used my team of videographers and editors.

Scan the QR code to watch "Put it in your ads."	SCAN ME

We pushed the boundaries a little. Why? Because it's harmless fun and hilarious to me.

In the next video, I created a character named "Pedro." Pedro is a Latino who can't pronounce the word "focus" correctly. Instead, it sounds like he's saying something profane, offensive, and ridiculously awesome. I created this ad to promote one of my products, where I teach entrepreneurs how to create funny ads to bring in more sales and leads for their business!

**Scan the QR code
to watch my
Pedro character
in "Focus."**

🔲 SCAN ME

When creating characters for yourself, ask yourself what special skills you have. What kind of character do you feel comes easily to you? When I did Ads Dominatrix, I happened to be able to do a decent Russian accent and could already naturally pretend to abuse people. (not proud of that, but it is what it is) For "Pedro," I could do a Latin Accent and I'm Hispanic, so it was natural to head in that direction. What special skills do you have that you could incorporate into a character?

**Here's another ad that I created
for Funnel Hacking Live. where
I played three different characters
with three different accents!
This is very similar to my "Funny Ad #2,"
but I use three characters instead of two!**

🔲 SCAN ME

Here's the thing: life throws us curveballs. Some are funny, and some... aren't. But guess what? You can turn even tough stuff into something hilarious and profitable.

For example, during my time as a webcam model, I experienced a lot of weird, uncomfortable situations. I even felt ashamed of what I did during that time, but those feelings were a waste. Instead, when I created Ads Dominatrix, I transformed a part of my past that once made me cringe, into something I could laugh about, profit from, and use to entertain audiences both on stage and online. That's the beauty of humor. It gives you your power back.

When you take a painful moment, laugh at it, and turn it into creative content that makes you money. You're not just surviving. You're thriving. You're saying, "This thing doesn't own me. I own it."

So next time you're stuck on a character, just look around. A costume, a memory, or even a random accent might spark an idea. You've got this, and who knows? Your next character might just be the star of your most viral and profitable ad yet.

MAKING YOUR CUSTOMER LAUGH
THE ENTIRE WAY

I finally gave my funny ads agency a name, *Laugh My Ads Off*. I tried to get *Kiss My Ads*, but the domain was taken. I had also considered *Open a Can of Whoop Ads* and other variations before I landed on *Laugh My Ads Off*.

We've made ads for a number of companies ranging from lead generation services to life coaches to painting instructors and beyond.

One of my favorite people to work with is Eric Beer, who runs a lead generation company. His business is kind of "boring," so he came to me to help make it fun and unforgettable for his audience. Eric teaches other entrepreneurs how to get started in lead gen, and we worked on everything for him. We did his ads, funnels, landing page videos, and even his webinar. His customers get to laugh on every single page during their entire buying journey! This is something fun I would highly recommend for you as well! I'll share a few of those samples of the videos!

In this ad that I am about to show you, you'll notice we "stacked" a number of things I've taught throughout this book:

- We have an attention-grabbing hook that pushes boundaries
- We cover the pain points of entrepreneurs. "Dancing on TikTok" and "working for a boss you hate."

- We created a fictional character: "The Grandma." (In this chapter, we obviously love using Grandma characters!)

Watch Eric Beer's "Grandma" ad.

Scan the QR code:

SCAN ME

We also filmed Eric's *landing page* video. It's the video people see *after* clicking on his ad and is on the website where people can register for his webinar. This is what I mean when I say that you can make customers laugh the entire way! Every click and every page all the way through the sale!

For the landing page video, we didn't want this to be one of those "yawn-and-click-away" videos. We wanted visitors to *actually enjoy* the experience of going through Eric's funnel. Because let's be honest, most people have no clue what "lead gen" even means.

So we turned it into a fun, educational video that doesn't put people to sleep. Why? Because humor doesn't just work in your ads! It works *everywhere* in your marketing. Even on landing pages! Keep 'em smiling, and they'll keep clicking.

Check out This Fun Landing Page Video from our shoot with Eric Beer.

SCAN ME

Here is another example of a much simpler landing page video I did for one of my own products. It just has one scene, and I even cast my 5-year-old son as my co-star! I love to create ads with him because he gets to learn about marketing, and we have a blast together. This is for a mini-course where I teach other entrepreneurs how to create an automated funnel that brings in cash flow around the clock. For landing page videos, the whole thing doesn't need to be a big, hilarious video. Just infuse a little humor here and there to keep people watching!

**Watch an example
of my landing page video
with a touch of humor!**

Scan the QR code:

SCAN ME

Last, here is an example of another landing page video I did for one of my membership programs. This is a monthly membership where I share content that is going viral every single week for business owners. Entrepreneurs can share this viral proven content on their own social media accounts and increase their views, exposure, and sales sometimes immediately! It's great because they don't have to create or shoot their own ads. They can just share already hilarious trending content that our team finds each week. It's a super awesome program and I wanted to do something really creative for this product. I used my 3-step formula in the form of a skit.

1. **Who is my customer?** Entrepreneurs who want to grow their business online with fun videos.
2. **What is their pain point?** They don't have a lot of time to be creating content or just don't want to.
3. **How can I exaggerate the pain point?** Create a "Fairy Headquarters" (aka "Sweatshop") where overworked fairies are forced to find trending content all day.

So I created this whole "Fairy HQ" in the conference building of my podcast studio, and the video was finished! I'm also a big fan of

The Office and their "interview" style segments so we decided to sprinkle some of that magic onto it as well!

**Watch my ridiculous
"Fairy HQ" landing
page video!**

Scan the QR code:

📱 SCAN ME

Adding humor to every step of your business isn't just fun for your customers. It's a game-changer for *you* too. Let's be real: burnout happens fast when things feel boring or repetitive. It's easy to think about quitting when there's no fun in the process.

People love to say, *"Enjoy the journey,"* but let's be honest, how are you supposed to enjoy it if you're bored out of your mind? Business can feel like a never-ending to-do list, but your marketing? That part can always be fun. And when you're having fun, it's a whole lot easier to keep going.

In everything I do, I'm always asking myself, *How can I make this more fun for everyone and for me?*

When I speak on stage, I spend an almost embarrassing number of hours weaving in funny stories and jokes just to keep people hooked. I sneak humor into my ads, landing page videos, and even the tiny bits of text on my websites and funnels. I also pack my webinars with stories, skits, and a healthy dose of ridiculousness. And guess what? It's been incredible, not just for my business but for my sanity too. So here's my advice: find ways to add humor to every step of your customer journey! From your ads, to your landing page videos, and your thank you pages! Your customers will love it!

And life's already full of enough pain points, like taxes, traffic, and stepping on yet another LEGO your kid "forgot" to clean up. Might as well laugh your way through it :)

FUNNY AD #9: HATERS CAN MAKE YOU RICH

Haters can actually be a goldmine for ad ideas. Let me share a funny story.

I was at this music conference where bands were performing for booking agents, hoping to score paid gigs. This one duo got up on stage and sang this super motivational song. It was catchy, everyone was loving it, and then they ended with the line: "Anybody can accomplish their *dreeeeeeams*... (pause) unless you're a girl."

I laughed so hard I thought I might pee my pants. The crowd erupted. It was so unexpected. That moment stuck with me.

So later, when comments like, "I don't trust women in business" started popping up on my posts, I couldn't help but find them hilarious. One guy even wrote to me, *"I don't trust anything that bleeds for a week and doesn't die."* (I'll admit, that one was hilarious)

Here's the thing: If the haters are right and women *do* suck at business, and I'm supposedly useless for one week out of the month, then doesn't that actually prove my methods work? I mean, if someone as incompetent as me can make millions, what's stopping anyone else?

I was so inspired by the "Women suck at business" comments that I decided to spoof Geico's "It's so easy a caveman could do it." In one of my ads, I created the slogan: "Make funny ads. It's so easy, even a girl can do it."

In the next ad, I kept the same theme, but I took it a little further and also chose to make fun of "Bro-Marketing." "Bro-Marketing" is where guys constantly show videos of themselves with fancy cars, girls, and whatever else to appeal to guys. And in many cases, those cars aren't even theirs.

I decided to do the same thing but using a jet that wasn't mine. I often create ads to target a very specific group. In Funny Ad #1 of this book, I targeted moms. In this next ad, I would target men. Both ads are for the same product but use different humor to appeal to different audiences. I figured men might find this video funny and women, maybe not so much. But the result? Actually, a lot of women liked it, but plenty entered my comment section to say it was tasteless and offensive. Guess that means they're *definitely* not buying... which is fine. I guess I won't be saving them a seat in my fake jet.

For months, this was the best-performing video ad I had. Funny thing is, this is probably the most hated ad I've ever put out. I'd say a good percentage of the people who watch it comment about how "not funny" it is. In fact, when I finished editing it, I almost didn't put it out there because I didn't even like it myself much.

Here's one of the most important things I've learned: You are NOT your customer. Your personal opinion about your content doesn't matter nearly as much as how your audience responds to it. And guess what? You don't need everyone to like you.

Even if a bunch of people hate your ad or claim to hate you personally, it doesn't matter. Like I've said before, success doesn't come from winning over the masses. It comes from getting a tiny percentage of viewers to buy. That's it! The truth is, most people could roll their eyes, leave snarky comments, or even think you're the worst, and you can *still* make a ton of money.

Oh, and by the way, I save the funniest negative comments in a special folder because, honestly, they're *pure gold*. Who knows? They might even inspire my next ad.

In fact, I had an idea I thought would be fun. I want to share some of the comments that I've gotten that were supposed to be a diss but were actually a compliment and put it in an ad. Here are a few for your enjoyment.

COMMENTS THAT WERE SUPPOSED TO BE "HURTFUL" BUT WERE ACTUALLY COMPLIMENTS

Mark Dawson · Follow
If you didn't look like a six year old I might listen to you.
[OBJ]

Hide   23w

So he's saying I look young. #blushing

Rebecca Stover
This is such a terrible add. Like no effort. No budget.

20h   Like   Reply   Send message   Hide

So this means I put in no effort, no budget, and made a "terrible" ad, yet I've made millions with it. #Winning

> **Michael D. Keeney** · Follow
> My God, please make a new commercial. Seeing this since 52 B.C. is obscene 😣
>
> Like   Reply   Hide   Send message   3h

So I have one ad that's been running for ages and is still profitable, and I don't have to make content every day? #yesplease

If you're worried that people will comment about how much they hate your ad or how awful you are... don't worry. They will. And trust me, I've heard it all (I've even gotten death threats). The secret is just to laugh it off, keep creating, keep testing, and keep going. The only real failure is stopping.

Your goal as a business owner isn't to win a "Best Comedian Ever" award. It's to make money. (Unless your goal *is* to win awards, in which case, congrats, you picked up the wrong book.)

The great thing is you can find inspiration everywhere, even in the people that don't like you. And especially if there is a recurring negative opinion about you, instead of fighting it, embrace it!

It reminds me of what Eminem does in his raps. He points out every bad thing someone could say about him, so there's nothing left for anyone else to use against him. It's genius, really. By owning the negativity, you take back all the power, and it can even turn into something creative and brilliant.

HOW I MADE $400K IN THREE DAYS
OF WORK

The entire foundation of my business, every sale, every milestone, every success comes down to this: fun, entertaining ads built my audience. And that audience made everything else possible.

If no one knows your products or services exist, you could have the cure for every disease in the world, and you would still have no sales.

Yet you could have a totally mediocre product, and if you have an audience, you could be a millionaire.

At one point, I made $400k in a single event that was held over just one weekend. I hosted a music conference, and it wasn't because I ran fancy marketing campaigns or spent thousands on ads. It was because I had already built an email list full of people who knew me, liked me, and trusted me. And that list? It existed because of the funny, viral ads I had been creating all along.

Let me show you how it all came together.

In my first successful online business, I had been running funny ads to promote my $19 books for musicians. But those ads weren't just about making quick sales, they were about building relationships and bringing in leads who actually *stuck around*. Over time, I grew an email list of around 40,000 buyers within about 18 months.

Now, let me clarify, these weren't just *followers*. Followers can be... meh. Just because someone hits the follow button doesn't mean they're ready to buy from you. They might just like your hair. But my email list? It wasn't a fan club. It was a **buyer's list.** A HIGH-QUALITY list of people with one thing in common: they all pulled out their credit cards and bought something from me.

And let me tell you, an email list of 40,000 *buyers* is worth WAY more than millions of followers who are just there because they think you're cute. Buyers have intent. Followers? They just watch. Big difference.

This list was my secret weapon.

I had joined Russell Brunson's Inner Circle Mastermind (A very cool group of entrepreneurs who all had made a minimum of a million dollars in sales), and started to learn from other amazing people who had built online businesses. I jumped on a call with my friend Robbie Summers (Hi Robbie!), and he said I should hold a music conference for musicians and sell tickets for $5,000 each.

Wait... what!??!?!

I knew I could completely change the lives of musicians, get them booked gigs, bring in booking agencies, record labels, managers, and all sorts of huge names, but I never really considered that I could sell a ticket for $5,000. But he asked me... if an artist signs with an agent there, what could they earn? I explained to him that I had earned hundreds of thousands of dollars myself just from one of the booking agents that would be attending my conference. So he explained that charging $5,000 was actually a steal. And he was right. I knew my offer was invaluable.

Now, here's the thing. I had a few amazing contacts, but I knew I could bring in big record labels even though I didn't have the connections at the time. We started marketing which labels would be there, and even though they weren't confirmed, I walked in faith. I knew if we sold tickets, I would be forced to make this incredible conference a success. (or be ruined forever. One or the other) I started reaching out to every record label, every booking agent, every manager, any amazing music contact and made it happen.

Now to sell tickets to the event, I didn't need to start from scratch. I didn't need to run new ads or host webinars. I simply sent a few emails to my list. That's it.

I had no affiliates, I didn't pay for any promotions, nothing.

We sold almost 80 tickets. That's nearly $400k in revenue for a three-day event. After covering event costs, we walked away with almost $350k profit. And we did it all without spending a dime on paid traffic.

Here's what really matters: I never could have pulled off a high-priced event like that without first building an audience. And I never would have built that audience without funny ads.

The magic formula I followed wasn't rocket science:

Funny Ads ➔ Build Audience ➔ Market Offers Forever ➔ Potential Lifetime Income

My final lesson to share with you? Once you've built an audience, **you're set.** You can keep creating and selling new offers to them for life! It's like planting a money tree. Keep watering it, and it keeps growing.

Your ability to earn is only limited by your own creativity.

That customer list you build is GOLD, and now you can reach them virtually for free now that they are in your community.

And what makes this all work? **TRAFFIC.**

And how did I get the traffic? **FUNNY ADS.**

When you have traffic, when you have people paying attention to what you're saying, you have power. And when you can build traffic profitably, and in a way that actually makes people LIKE YOU, you create a brand that people trust and WANT to buy from.

Looking back, I didn't realize the full impact of what I was doing. I just followed the steps. I created funny content, built my email list, and showed up consistently. And that's how I built a business that changed my life.

The conference itself was more than just profitable. It was deeply rewarding. Attendees left in tears, formed lifelong friendships, signed deals, and booked tours. It wasn't just an event; it was a transformational experience.

But none of that would have happened without funny ads. Those ads built my audience. That audience built my business.

And it all started by making people laugh.

ENDING THOUGHTS

As I'm wrapping up this book, it's hitting me that most people don't make it this far. Honestly, most people aren't willing to sit through an entire book of nonsense like this.

But you did.

Maybe that makes you a big weirdo, just like me. Or maybe, deep down, you *love* the idea of making a total fool of yourself... while also making money doing it.

Either way, welcome to the club.

My intention was to share how a normal person facing challenges can always find a way to achieve whatever their definition of success is. I never wanted to grow up; I never wanted to stop being ridiculous in front of a camera, so I figured out how to turn it into a business. Regardless of your desires, you can build a life that allows you to do something you enjoy, too.

Whatever painful situations you experience, they don't have to hold you back or scar you. Those challenges can actually be what makes you successful.

I wouldn't have the success I have had if I hadn't been given the chance to fight my battle as a single mom building my business in that garage and on that farmland. If everything had been easy, what kind of story would I even have to tell? A pretty boring one. What skills would I have been forced to build? Not many. I'm excited for you and your story, even if you feel like it's a train wreck at times.

I like to think of all our challenges as a gift. Granted, some gifts are more like a surprise root canal on your birthday, but hey, it's still character-building, right?

In all seriousness, though, I wouldn't change a thing.

Opportunities are everywhere. Where someone else might've seen an old piece of trash toilet sitting in the backyard, I saw the potential for a video ad. That ad made me a lot of money and inspired me to make more silly videos simply because I chose to view it as an opportunity.

These opportunities are all around you. It's up to you to make the most of every situation, good and bad.

Always remember to find humor in *everything*. All the pain, all the bad times, all the things that you felt were going to kill you. Life can really punch you in the face, but don't ever let it take away your ability to laugh at how ridiculous you look with that black eye.

Put yourself out there! The world needs to know that your products and services exist if you want to grow your business. And not everyone's going to think you're funny. But here's the reminder: you only need a tiny fraction of people to find you amusing enough to check out your offer and then an even tinier fraction of *those* people to buy. That's it. Most people can think you're awful, and you can still make more money than you could dream of.

Also, building a targeted audience that wants what you're selling can be the most important thing you ever commit to doing. With an audience, you can create and sell things that provide a great livelihood for you and the people you care about for the rest of your life. And humor is the best way to attract that audience in a huge and impactful way.

And last, I'll leave with one final thought.

When I was younger, I found myself in physically abusive relationships, dragged by my hair across the floor and up steps, thrown into walls, and choked to the point that my whole body ached. And it happened again and again because I didn't value myself enough to walk away. I was too weak to leave... and way too broke to feel like I *could* leave.

There was one day when this particular person had their hand wrapped around my throat. I remember even my legs were hurting because of how hard he was choking me. I somehow managed to get him out of the car, and he started punching my windows to try to get back in. I remember his face looking as though the devil lived in his eyes. He didn't look like a person anymore. I didn't open the door. Instead, I drove off with the tiny bit of gas I had in my old Jeep and stopped at this old, busted Motel 6. This was in Albuquerque, NM, where gunshots at night and meth houses were all normal. There was a big sign that said $34 a night. I knew that, with tax and everything, it'd be a little over $40 to stay the night.

I had no money. I had no jobs coming up. I had no friends, and I didn't know what to do. I turned my car back around and went right back to his house. The rest of the evening didn't get any better.

I couldn't afford a measly $40 to leave that situation. Not only that, but I also felt helpless and didn't hold myself very high. Even if I had the $40, maybe I still just wouldn't have valued myself enough or respected myself enough to leave that situation.

I say all of this because when people say money doesn't buy happiness, I truly believe it's only because that person was never poor enough to see that it certainly does. I am a WHOLE lot happier now than I have money. It's not even comparable. And when you're not earning, you can easily feel worthless and not valuable enough to leave terrible situations.

Having money has brought me safety, not just for myself but for my son and my family, and has allowed us to experience beautiful things in life we never would have experienced otherwise.

More importantly, my son will never have to experience what it's like to have to go back to an abusive situation because he can't afford a Motel 6.

Money buys safety, it buys impact, it pays your family's rent when they can't cover it, and it buys a means for you to be able to leave any situation that hurts you without you having to think about how you're going to cover your basic needs.

Not only that, but to make money, I had to bring real value to the world. I've written books and created coaching programs that have impacted thousands of lives. It wasn't just about earning money. I gained confidence, self-respect, and a sense of purpose while helping others. Seeing how my products changed other people's lives for the better brought purpose into my own life and made all the difference.

Money can buy a whole lot of happiness, and you should get a whole lot of it.

Furthermore, there is also nothing admirable about suffering, and being poor doesn't make you a good person. This is a mentality that has plagued us and made so many people feel better about not living up to their potential. I had a friend who always told me that if I wanted to make a lot of money, that must be "the devil" talking to me. But all I could think was: *If I believe I "should" be poor, that I "should" struggle, and that I "should" watch my family suffer, wouldn't "that" be more of a devilish idea?*

Why does life have to be miserable to prove you're a good person? Since when is happiness a sin?

Go out, create something that can change the lives of others, and pursue it with everything you have. Your children's safety and happiness could be at stake.

The person you become will dramatically change, and *that* will be the thing that ends up making you successful or not.

When I decided to write this book, my intention wasn't just to share with people how I've used humor in my ads, but actually how I've used humor in my WHOLE LIFE and how you can too. I just happened to channel the energy into online marketing, but you can use it in all aspects of your life.

I hope that whatever you've been through in your life, you can find the humor in it and shift whatever may have been plaguing you into something that can drive you and those around you into laughter. The lens through which I have chosen to look at life has helped me through the hardest times. I am happy to say that my life is dramatically different from those darker days.

You can see life as an incredible adventure, or you can find a million excuses for why you'll never succeed. It all depends on the lens you choose to look through. There's always someone out there who's done more than you have with less than you have. So, I hope you go out into the world, and instead of focusing on reasons you *can't* achieve your dreams, focus on all the reasons you *can*. And if you ever find yourself sleeping in a garage, just remember, you can still build a million-dollar business with as little as a toilet and a cell phone. Trust me on that one.

For a little fun, here's a song I wrote called *Young Soul*. You might recognize some of the lyrics from the stories in this book. Consider it the soundtrack to my chaos. Just remember, when life feels like a fire, the only way out is to keep going through it.

SCAN ME

HOW WE CAN WORK TOGETHER AND WHERE TO GO FROM HERE

Here are a few ways we can keep working together, or you can continue learning from me!

1. **Get my Course:** Get instant access to my video tutorials, ready-to-go scripts, and a magical tool I created that will WRITE YOUR FUNNY ADS FOR YOU in seconds. Yes, you'll basically be a comedic genius without even trying.

Scan the QR code to learn more and let the laughs (and sales) begin.

2. **Join me LIVE:** Join me in a LIVE multi-day training where I'll teach you how to create hilarious ads that actually bring in sales.

I write funny ads for *select* businesses LIVE, on the spot, no scripts, no safety net. You'll get to submit your ads for my (very honest) feedback and critiques. We'll hold contests, give out ridiculous prizes, and probably laugh until we cry.

Scan the QR code with your phone to *join the challenge, and let's make some magic happen.*

3. **We Create Funny Ads for Businesses:** On occasion, my team and I work with select businesses to create funny, attention-grabbing ads. We're very selective, but if you think we'd be a great fit, we'd love to hear from you.

Scan the QR code to apply:

Want to partner with me to earn commissions promoting my products to your audience? Scan the QR code to check out my current promos and apply to be an affiliate for my current offers. Get paid to share cool stuff!

THANK YOU FOR READING MY BOOK!

DOWNLOAD YOUR FREE GIFTS!

Just to say thanks for buying and reading my book, I'd like to give you a free bonus training below. This is how I created silly videos that brought in millions of views and millions in sales. I even cover a handful of ways you can make easy, funny ads for your business too, even if your business is boring, even if you're not creative or funny at all, and even if you have no idea where to start!

For the Free Training, Scan Below

I appreciate your interest in my book and value your feedback as it helps me improve future versions of this book. I would appreciate it if you could leave your invaluable review on Amazon.com. Thank you!

www.ingramcontent.com/pod-product-compliance
Lightning Source LLC
Chambersburg PA
CBHW070702190326
41458CB00046B/6812/J